YOGA FOR GOLFERS

YOGA
FOR
GOLFERS

A UNIQUE MIND-BODY APPROACH TO GOLF FITNESS

KATHERINE ROBERTS

McGraw·Hill

New York   Chicago   San Francisco   Lisbon   London   Madrid   Mexico City
Milan   New Delhi   San Juan   Seoul   Singapore   Sydney   Toronto

The McGraw·Hill Companies

Library of Congress Cataloging-in-Publication Data

Roberts, Katherine J., 1962–
     Yoga for golfers : a unique mind-body approach to golf fitness / by
Katherine Roberts.
          p.   cm.
     Includes bibliographical references.
     ISBN 0-07-142870-4
     1. Golf—Training.   2. Yoga.   3. Physical fitness.   I. Title.

GV979.T68 R63   2005
796.357—dc22   2004007943

The Yoga for Golfers program is designed to offer a safe, effective yoga practice for varying levels of flexibility and fitness. Intensify your yoga practice gradually, acknowledging your current level of fitness. If you have specific medical conditions such as high blood pressure, hip or knee replacements, arthritis, or chronic pain, be very focused on moving gradually in and out of the poses. Before beginning this or any other exercise program, obtain written approval from your physician. It is important to move very slowly and gently in each pose. Stop if you experience any discomfort or pain.

Yoga for Golfers includes photos of Paul Trittler, a *Golf Magazine* Top 100 teacher and Director of Instruction for the Kostis-McCord Learning Center in Scottsdale, Arizona.

     5 6 7 8 9 0   QPD/QPD   3 2 1 0 9 8 7 6

ISBN 0-07-142870-4

Interior photos by Tony Roberts

McGraw-Hill books are available at special quantity discounts to use as premiums and sales promotions, or for use in corporate training programs. For more information, please write to the Director of Special Sales, Professional Publishing, McGraw-Hill, Two Penn Plaza, New York, NY 10121-2298, or contact your local bookstore.

This book is printed on acid-free paper.

For my mother:

thank you for your unwavering support

and unconditional love.

For my father:

thanks, Dad. Nothing can replace our

Sunday afternoons on the putting green together.

I miss you more than words can say.

CONTENTS

Contents

PREFACE

As a lifelong golfer, I am honored to be writing a book about the game I have loved for many years and the sport that has been a binding thread in my family for five decades.

I have always been an avid athlete, playing many sports, with a consistent commitment to physical fitness. Years ago I discovered yoga by playing a round with a new friend, a woman who was a five handicap golfer. At the time I was playing to a twenty-four handicap and I wanted what she had! Oddly enough, though she was a marathon runner and avid golfer, my friend's yoga experience had a dramatic effect on her golf performance. This friend became my primary yoga teacher for the next six years. I now play to a sixteen!

When I served as the yoga instructor at some of the top golf and spa resorts in the country, my yoga students were avid golfers, and they began to experience similar benefits to their golf game. It was a light-bulb moment—yoga and golf: the perfect combination. After studying the mechanics of the golf swing and interviewing many PGA professionals, I began to compile a yoga sequence specific to a golfer's needs. The physical, mental, and life lessons of yoga are the perfect correlation to the game of golf.

I am honored to share the many gifts that yoga offers. Whether you come to yoga to experience the benefits in golf or in life, *enjoy*!

ACKNOWLEDGMENTS

As I followed my path of bringing yoga and golf together, educating the golf community about the benefits of yoga has been a labor of love. Five years ago I arrived at the PGA Merchandise Show in Las Vegas with poster, brochures, and yoga mat in tow. With the support of more people than I can mention in this book, the Yoga for Golfers program has become a well-known, accepted form of golf conditioning. I am so grateful to so many people in and out of the golf industry for their assistance.

There are a few individuals I must mention by name: my yoga teachers, Myra Lewin and Ana Forrest, who keep me grounded and committed. Thank you also to the following individuals whose insights, knowledge of the game, and belief in my work has been invaluable: Gary McCord, Peter Kostis, Paul Trittler, Ron Riemer, David Manougian, and Tony Roberts. Special thanks to my agent, John Monteleone, and my editor, Mark Weinstein. Paul Chek, of the C.H.E.K. Institute, and Jeff Banaszak, of Back 9 Fitness, contributed their extensive knowledge of golf biomechanics.

Thank you to our yoga students, Paul Trittler, Mark LeGault, and Andy DiSabatino, and to the GrayHawk Golf Club in Scottsdale, Arizona, which provided a remarkably beautiful background for our photos. Appreciation goes to my dogs, Shana and Shanti, who remained at my side (or lying at my feet) regardless of the time of day or night.

And, most important, thanks to my husband, Mark, whose incredible intelligence, wit, and love keep my heart shining.

INTRODUCTION

Golf has always been a part of my life. Growing up in Philadelphia, my father was an avid golfer, and my mother played on a golf team. I remember with love the sounds of metal cleats on concrete that symbolized the completion of my father's round. I knew he was only moments away and a hug from him was soon to follow. I also remember the endless hours of listening to my parents and their friends recapping the day's events on the golf course—closest to the pin, the putt that got away, and the long drives off the tee. I was amazed at how they could remember every detail. Their lives—personally, professionally, and socially—centered around the game of golf.

I would like to share a story of my father's about a golfing acquaintance of his. This gentleman (let's call him Larry) was known around town as a "rabid" golfer.

During a round, Larry's group was just behind my father's foursome. Although it was unlikely that he could have seen my father sinking putt after putt, Larry certainly must have heard the cheers of my father's compatriots as he dazzled them with his skill. After the round, Larry heard of my father's success on the greens and was sure it was the putter itself and not my father's talent. Larry, who was a very wealthy man, offered my father $1,000 for the putter. My father, who had five children to feed at home, was more than happy to take Larry's money.

Not more than a week later, Larry and his foursome were

playing in front of my father's foursome. Apparently, Larry was not having the same success with the putter as my father had experienced, and he was becoming exceedingly frustrated that his investment had been made in vain.

On the eighteenth hole, Larry missed yet another short putt. There was a loud yell, and my father witnessed his putter flying through the air and landing in the pond that bordered the green. Larry finally realized what most golfers have not yet grasped—you cannot *buy* a better golf game.

YOGA FOR GOLFERS

THEORIES OF YOGA: BREAKING OLD STEREOTYPES

The practice of yoga, which originated in India over five thousand years ago, has transformed millions of lives all over the world. In Sanskrit the word *yoga* was originally found in the *Vedas*, the most ancient scripture known to mankind. Yoga means "union" and refers to the connection of the body and mind. There are many traditional yogis (a man who practices yoga is a *yogin*; a woman is a *yogini*) who still maintain this time-honored, conventional yoga practice. Yoga's earliest esoteric philosophies are powerful tools applicable to everyday modern living.

Traditionally, yoga consists of physical postures or poses called *asanas*, breathing exercises, chanting, and meditation. The relationship among these components forms a concrete foundation with which one can cultivate more health through physical, mental, and spiritual inner peace. Yoga enables one to be fully present, focused, and consciously aware. With practice this connection of the mind and body becomes naturally instinctive.

A common fallacy about yoga is that you need to bend your body like a pretzel, burn incense, and chant to achieve yoga's full benefits. These misconceptions are rooted in images of ancient ashrams and traditional yoga practices. Recently, a more modern version of yoga has emerged, accommodating Western desires

and gaining universal acceptance. For many Western practitioners, yoga has become a form of physical exercise, one that provides tremendous benefits for the body as well as the mind. In America and around the world, yoga has quickly become the fastest growing movement in fitness. Yoga studios are opening in metropolitan areas as well as in the heartland, health clubs, corporations, and government agencies.

Yoga's benefits cannot be overstated. Physically, yoga has been linked to reductions in heart disease and decreases in the symptoms of arthritis and osteoporosis. Cancer patients use yoga to offset the effects of chemotherapy. Pregnancy and delivery are eased by specially designed prenatal yoga classes. Through deep yogic breathing, asthma sufferers find relief. Yoga has been proven to reduce depression, increase concentration, and manage stress levels. Yoga is offered in many school systems, providing children with increased self-esteem, focus, and direction.

Yoga's gifts are available to everyone. I commend you for taking the first steps toward experiencing what millions of people have already discovered.

TRADITIONAL YOGA VERSUS YOGA FOR GOLFERS

Most traditional yoga practices incorporate the physical practice of yoga poses, meditation, and breathing with ethical guiding principles. Divided into eight categories, the eight limbs of yoga are the foundation or trunk of the tree of yoga. Knowledge of and reverence for yoga's foundation are important to understanding its evolution. For traditional yogis, the journey toward enlightenment includes this eight-limbed path of mind, body, and spirit integration.

1. Foundations of ethics toward the world: *yamas*
2. Our personal conduct, personal discipline: *niyamas*
3. The physical practice of yoga: *asana*
4. The practice of breathing: *pranayama*
5. Withdrawing from the senses; moving toward internal awareness: *pratyahara*
6. Concentration of the mind: *dharana*
7. Meditation: *dhyana*
8. Enlightenment: *samadhi*

Each path should be approached with an open mind, and each offers many life lessons that we integrate into the Yoga for Golfers program, applying the principles both on and off the golf course.

The term *hatha yoga* (among the most well-known styles of yoga) is the umbrella covering various physical modalities, each with its own philosophies, methodologies, and teaching paradigms. The *Iyengar* method of yoga focuses on alignment by using props such as straps, blocks, and blankets to place students into a pose. Generally, the poses are held for one to five minutes. *Ashtanga* or *power* yoga (which is the Western adaptation) is extremely physically intense. This style emphasizes a continuous flow of postures, moving from one to another. The sequence of postures rarely deviates from the traditional, and requires strength and flexibility. Typically, the poses are held for five breaths. *Bikram*, or hot-room, yoga links twenty-six poses together with short resting periods between the sitting poses. The room is often heated to over 100 degrees on the theory that warm muscles will stretch beyond their normal capacity, thus increasing flexibility. *Kundalini* yoga involves breathing exercises as well as the classic postures, coordinated with meditation and chanting. This style is intended to release the kundalini, or life force energy in the body. *Restorative* yoga is intended to bring the body back to its original, whole state of health. With the use of props, blankets, blocks, chairs, and straps, the body is supported, allowing the student to rest in the poses for extended periods of time. This practice provides tremendous overall health benefits.

While we respect and honor the over-five-thousand-year-old path of yoga, the Yoga for Golfers program slightly modifies certain aspects of the traditional practice. This book incorporates a Western approach to yoga. We have chosen to modify or delete the Sanskrit text, instead providing the English translation when applicable. We offer simplified breathing techniques to enhance concentration and increase endurance on the golf course. Meditation is practiced to calm the mind, focus, and visualize the desired golf-specific outcome.

We use cutting-edge golf-swing biomechanical processes and apply yoga principles to our training paradigm. A specifically developed sequencing of poses offers the most efficient, comprehensive training regimen for golf performance.

By offering modifications for each pose, we accommodate varying levels of fitness and golf abilities, embracing a wide range of populations. Regardless of your age, physical challenges, or flexibility, *Yoga for Golfers* offers the tools to begin, maintain, and advance your yoga practice, achieving results on and off the golf course.

Yoga for Golfers incorporates flexibility, strength, balance, core conditioning, and breathing awareness, teaching focus, relaxation, and visualization techniques. The sequence of postures is carefully designed to meet the golfer's needs. Relaxation techniques are used to quiet the overactive mind and teach visualization tools, essential for golf performance.

Flexibility, the most obvious physical requirement for golfers that can be achieved through yoga, is a core component in the *Yoga for Golfers* program. Flexibility increases your range of motion in the golf swing, reduces swing faults caused by short, tight muscles, and produces more club head speed. Some poses are practiced in a dynamic or fluid sequence of movements, while others are held in place. Using golf biomechanical training paradigms, we address the specific needs of golfers.

Strength is achieved in yoga by flexing or engaging the muscles. We use the force of gravity and your own body weight to build strength. Described as the oldest form of isometric strength training, certain yoga postures are weight bearing, increasing muscular strength and endurance. Long, lean muscles are developed, increasing strength without restricting the golf swing. In addition, when certain joints experience "hyperflexibility," more functional strength-building modalities are recommended. A clear description of the muscles affected and the direct golf benefit are provided for each pose.

Balance is a fundamental aspect of the yoga practice. As the body ages, the nerve endings in the spine become less efficient, affecting balance and proprioception (the ability to understand body position in space). For our purposes, balance refers to the physical, the musculoskeletal system often thrown out of balance by the golf swing. Balance also translates to feeling grounded or connected to the earth. The Sanskrit term *apana viyu* describes the downward energy of the body. In golf, balance in your stance and throughout the entire swing plane is vital for a consistent, reliable golf swing.

Core conditioning is one of the most important aspects of golf performance. Core conditioning, which involves strengthening the essential abdominal and back muscles, is a critical element for golf success. Working the core supports longevity in the sport. Working the core improves posture at address, reduces fatigue in the golf swing and putting stance, and is a direct correlation to trunk rotation. The term *uddiyana bandha*, or "flying upward," refers to energy and strength moving from just below the navel upward to the head. Becoming accustomed to incorporating this type of strength in the core during your preshot routine brings more stability to your posture. We often refer to "drawing the navel toward the spine," a common yoga principle that will become second nature. In addition, you may lose weight around the midsection while strengthening not only the abdominal muscles but the erector spinae, or low-back muscles, as well. Developing core abdominal strength has a clinically proven correlation with low-back health. Simply put, to stay balanced and hit the ball longer and with less fatigue, you must exercise your core.

Breathing awareness is the most important element in the practice of yoga. The quality of breath has a direct correlation with the quality of the pose and the quietness of the mind. Proper breathing increases blood flow to the muscles and increases core body temperature. Deep breathing enhances the ability to hold poses, thus increasing endurance. Certain yoga postures coordinate breathing and movement (as in dynamic stretching) or long slow breaths while you hold the pose (as in static stretching). On the golf course when the body and mind are stressed during challenging shots, bad lies, and first-tee jitters, the breathing becomes jerky, rapid, and strained. By practicing long, slow, deep breaths during the yoga practice, breathing awareness becomes second nature—an immediate tool to "feel" your game. When the body and mind are under pressure, either in a yoga pose or in the golf swing, erratic, shallow breathing is the first sign of stress. By providing applicable tools for incorporating breathing into your preshot routine, we will enhance rhythm, tempo, and fluidity in your swing.

Focus, meditation, and visualization are essential tools on the golf course. Tiger Woods has been quoted as saying he visualizes every shot in his mind before he steps up to the ball. An example of the power of focus is a story I heard about Jack Nicklaus. Jack was putting for the lead in a major when a dog ran out onto the green. Jack proceeded to sink the putt without hesitation. Later, when asked if he was distracted by the dog, his response was, "What dog?" Now that is concentration! Breathing, one-pointed attention, and *asanas*, or yoga poses, are the foundations for developing a meditation practice.

At the end of each practice we take time to rest. This pose is called *savasana*, which means "corpse pose." Lying on your back, you allow your body and mind to become completely relaxed. This period in the practice is the most important and should never be missed. When the mind and body are relaxed, one becomes receptive to subliminal messages and focus techniques.

We also address the more spiritual life lessons of yoga that have a direct impact on golf. Letting go of the outcome, acceptance, fear, commitment, and freedom are metaphors for golf and life.

Let's get started, because your body doesn't get a mulligan!

3

WHAT TO EXPECT FROM THE YOGA FOR GOLFERS FITNESS PROGRAM

As golfers we are constantly challenged by requirements placed on the body and mind. For golf performance, the golfer is required to execute an explosive movement, involving almost every muscle in the body, from a static position. His mind must stay calm and focused and calculate the next shot and club selection with precision. At the same time, golfers are bombarded with external influences such as weather, slow play, and injuries. Oh yes, and for most of us this is recreation! *Yoga for Golfers* provides the necessary tools to enhance your golf performance for both body and mind. Each pose is explained in detail, offering modifications for varying levels of fitness.

Improved Flexibility and Strength

Successful professional and amateur golfers share similar physical skills—flexibility and strength. Practicing yoga dramatically increases flexibility, enabling the body to move more easily through a full range of motion. Many golfers ask if they can build strength by practicing yoga. Absolutely! Holding the poses while fully extending and contracting the muscles is a form of isometric strength training. In yoga we use the force of gravity against our own body weight; this creates weight-bearing, strength-building exercises. The biomechanical portion of this book explains how the musculoskeletal system functions during the various phases of the golf swing. Our baseline rotation test, forward fold test, and hip-extension testing determine a baseline of mobility, providing you the ability to qualify and quantify your progress. Increasing distance and accuracy off the tee are a few of the many correlations of flexibility and strength conditioning to golf.

Enhanced Breathing Awareness

One of the oldest tricks in golf is to throw your partner off by asking him when he breathes in his golf swing. When do you breathe? Do you breathe or hold your breath? If you are one of the few who know, when does your breathing become compromised? Any stress we experience on the golf course—first shot, tight lie, or any shot that creates anxiety—can cause the body to respond with breath retention (holding the breath) or hyperventilation (rapid, shallow, uncontrollable breathing).

The physiological effect of holding the breath is a loss of blood flow to the extremities, including the brain. Can you effectively execute the golf swing when the blood is leaving the extremities, including your brain and hands? Yoga incorporates continuous deep, diaphragmatic breathing, allowing the process to become intuitive.

In the breathing section, we will practice sport-specific applied breathing exercises to incorporate into your preshot routine. Remember Annika Sorenstam on the first tee of the Colonial? The only way she could execute her tee shot under that stressful condition was to breathe! Controlling the breath corresponds to controlled heart rate. The breath has a direct effect on relieving tension in the golf swing and improves rhythm and tempo—reducing the number-one reason for swing flaws.

Quieter Mind

In the ancient yoga text, the *Yoga Sutras*, the first sentence describes the purpose of yoga: "Cessation of fluctuation of the mind." This refers to one's ability to keep the mind calm and focused on the task at hand, while all other thoughts seem to drift out of sight. How many times have you stood on the tee box staring at a water hazard and saying to yourself, "Please, please, please, don't hit it into the water"? Usually the next sound is a big splash! By moving into the poses and holding them for an extended period of time, we learn to stay completely focused. This sense of being present, conscious, and aware facilitates concentration. Moving the mind into a "zonelike" state while maintaining full awareness is the purpose of yoga. A quiet mind is open to subliminal and conscious suggestions. Practicing visualization techniques will create the power to manifest your intention and your desired golf outcome into reality. Developing a quieter mind will increase concentration and visualization capabilities.

Improved Overall Fitness

Strength, flexibility, balance, core strength, and cardiovascular endurance are components of sound physical fitness. *Yoga for Golfers* provides a comprehensive approach to all these facets of fitness. Developing strength will provide additional, consistent power in your swing. A healthy, fit body is less prone to injury. (When the body is in pain, you will instinctively anticipate the physical reaction and you will not swing with freedom.) Muscle endurance is increased; recovery time is decreased. Improving your overall fitness reduces risk of injury and recovery time.

Increased Sense of Balance

For the purposes of this book, we will define balance in two ways—musculoskeletal balance and balance in posture and weight distribution throughout the golf swing. The golf swing, by virtue of its biomechanical requirements, creates an imbalance in the body. Golf is often referred to as a "one-sided sport." By holding poses on the restricted or less-flexible parts of the body, we begin to bring more balance to the overused parts of the body. At the same time, we will pay attention to the areas of the body that are already flexible and work to create more functional strength in those areas. Practicing balancing poses supports awareness of weight distribution and facilitates increased concentration. Balance affects spinal movement in the swing, club control, and weight distribution. Tom Lehman has said his commitment to physical conditioning allows him "to swing as hard as possible and remain balanced."

4

IMPROVE YOUR GOLF PERFORMANCE AND OVERALL HEALTH WITH YOGA

A recent letter from a new Yoga for Golfers student sums up its numerous benefits for health and well-being:

Katherine,

I started using your DVD about three weeks ago. I turn forty-nine in April and all of a sudden I'm playing the best golf of my life. Some other things are occurring as well. I am losing inches around my midsection. I have a lot more energy and I feel better. I now know what it feels like to stand with the correct posture and I'm doing so. I am healthier.

I travel over 100,000 air miles per year and find it very difficult to always find good workout facilities. All I do now is get up a half hour earlier and do Yoga for Golfers.

In closing, thank you for developing this great product. It has already had a profound impact on my life.

Thanks,

Bob H., Oregon

One of the greatest gifts of yoga is its tremendous health benefit. What does good health mean to you? It is important to be clear regarding your intentions, expectations, and goals for your health through the yoga practice. Take the time to write down your current golf challenges, physical and mental. Be specific. Include, for example, that you want to work on your balance in order to improve a swing that "breaks down." Or note a physical component, such as a need to increase club control with the hands, or any mental challenges, such as a desire to improve your concentration. This will help you develop a baseline, a starting point from which to chart your progress.

A road map to the desired destination is the best way to understand your goal. (And don't be afraid to ask for directions!) Perhaps your aim will be to increase your physical strength and flexibility. Look forward to managing challenges with greater ease, to breathe when you feel pressure, and to have more vitality and endurance than before. Perhaps you intend to hit the golf ball with less tension, to be more present on the greens, and to have more joy in your golf game. Expect to let go of old habits that no longer serve your health and well-being. Take time for yourself. If you allow it to, yoga transforms the body and mind.

In the *Yoga for Golfers* sequencing of poses, you have the opportunity to select a sequence based on time; for example, a fifteen-minute sequence in your hotel room or locker room, or a forty-minute sequence for your living room, or a sequence on the golf course right before the round. The following are golf-specific and health-specific benefits you can derive from this program. These are delineated by body area.

Neck and Traps, or Upper-Shoulder Poses

Golf benefit: Maintain steady head position with comfort.
Health benefit: Yoga postures such as shoulder shrugs, neck releasers, and arm extensions relieve neck and shoulder tension. We will learn to create a slight "traction" in the neck, relieving compression in the cervical vertebrae. This area is a common

place to hold your stress. Yoga relieves tension in the neck and top of the shoulders.

Hand and Wrist Poses

Golf benefit: Club control throughout the entire swing. This is your only connection to the club.

Health benefit: Yoga postures reduce pain caused by repetitive hand and wrist strain by providing strengthening poses and traction in the joints. Cocking the wrists during the takeaway and at the top of the swing, carpal tunnel syndrome, and the onset of arthritis can cause pain in the hands and wrists.

Shoulder and Upper-Back Poses
(Rotator Cuff, Rhomboids, and Thoracic Spine)

Golf benefit: Supports increased shoulder turn, reduces risk of rotator-cuff injury, supports club control at the top of the swing.

Health benefit: Yoga postures such as rhomboid stretches, chest openers, eagle arms, and downward dogs release tension. Yoga supports correct posture and relieves upper-back pain that results from a sedentary lifestyle. Note: Be conscious of the way you carry your golf bag, briefcase, or purse. Proper placement can affect posture and neck and shoulder strain.

Erector Spinae, or Low-Back Muscle Poses

Golf benefit: Increases range of motion and power. Supports a consistent spine angle and repeatable swing pattern.

Health benefit: Yoga postures such as twists facilitate synovial or spinal fluid in the joints, acting as a natural lubricant to ease back pain. Postures increase blood flow to the muscles, reducing fatigue, pain, and the onset of sciatica. Yoga supports proper posture, reduces fatigue, and relieves low-back pain. Note: Pay attention to your sleeping position. This may have a direct effect on your low-back health.

Core-Conditioning Poses

Golf benefit: Initiates rotation of the trunk for an increased range of motion. Supports control of the golf swing and generates power by increasing the X factor.

Health benefit: Developing a strong core supports a straight spine, reduces the onset of back pain, and keeps the internal organs supported. Yoga decreases the onset of postural changes associated with aging.

Hip Flexors/Psoas Poses

Golf benefit: Stretching and strengthening the hip flexors and psoas enables greater power and extension in the finish position of the swing and allows the glutes to engage, generating more power, club head speed, and distance off the tee.

Health benefit: Decreases the onset of low-back pain caused by spinal compression from sitting at a desk or riding in the golf cart.

Lower Body: Quadriceps and Hamstring Poses

Golf benefit: Quad and hamstring health supports proper knee flexion at address. Strong and flexible legs support the body's ability to maintain a strong foundation and balance during compromising lies. Yoga helps you stay "down on the ball."

Health benefit: Yoga postures use contraction and extension theories of movement, creating strength as well as flexibility in the legs. You will experience greater ease of movement and support in the back.

Knee, Calf, and Foot Poses

Golf benefit: Greater stabilization and balance, and a sense of being grounded to the earth. Effects push-off power and weight distribution in the finish position. Supports balance in a bad lie and increases endurance when walking the course.

Health benefit: Relieves pain in the arches and some plantar fascia issues. Restorative yoga poses reduce the effects of varicose veins, relieving inflammation in the joints of the lower extremities.

You now possess the information and opportunity to benefit your golf game and overall health!

5

WHY CONDITION FOR GOLF?

Every golfer wants to play better golf. For many, golf is a chance to relax, relieve stress, do business, and exercise. But the wish to lower one's personal handicap and improve one's score is present in even the laid-back recreational golfer. The most common method used to achieve this goal is a combination of professional lessons and diligent practice. Although this approach seems logical, it is the very reason many golfers end up injured and rarely reach their potential. Why? Simply because few golfers associate the need for improved physical conditioning with their quest for improved performance.

The average golfer tends to take up the game at an age when he or she is no longer racing around a sports field, nor actively participating in other competitive or physically demanding sports. Golf is generally viewed as a game of technical skill rather than an athletic event, requiring less exertion than most other sports. Unfortunately, this common misperception all too often results in injury and/or premature performance plateaus. The reason is very simple: golf is a highly athletic event! To put this in perspective, consider that the head of a golf club can travel over 100 miles per hour, an effort comparable to pitching a baseball. Or the fact that amateur golfers achieve approximately 90 percent of their peak muscle activity when driving a golf ball. This is the same lifting intensity as picking up a weight that can only be lifted four times before total fatigue sets

in. Yet golfers fail to consider that they strike the ball an average of thirty to forty times a game with comparable intensity! This level of exertion and muscle activation raises golf to a level similar to sports such as football, hockey, and martial arts. The difference is that these athletes use a physical training program as an integral part of their preparation for their sport, whereas most golfers do not.

A Word on Injury and Pain

When an athlete is hurt, careful consideration must be given to the cause of the injury. Often patients are looking for the "quick fix." Doctors and therapists may focus on removing the pain rather than addressing the root cause of the problem. When the removal of pain is perceived as the cure, though, problems are sure to ensue. Recurring pain in the back, shoulder, knee, wrist, and elbow is much too common among golfers.

- At any given time, as many as 30 percent of all professional golfers are playing injured.
- Fifty-three percent of male and 45 percent of female golfers suffer from back pain.
- Those who play golf and participate in another sport are 40 percent more likely to develop back pain than those who just play golf.

By following a carefully designed exercise program such as Yoga for Golfers, the risk of injury may be reduced. Additionally, a golfer already suffering from an injury will have much greater success returning to the game if his program addresses the underlying cause of the problem.

Is Technology Lowering Golf Scores?

Have you noticed that the scores achieved by the world's top golf pros have hardly changed in the past thirty years? For example, a quick look through the *1995 Golfer's Handbook* reveals the following:

- The U.S. Masters Championship was won in 1939 with a winning score of 279.
- In 1994, fifty-five years later, the U.S. Masters Championship was won with the same score of 279.
- The 1958 U.S. PGA Championship was won with a score of 276.
- The same tournament thirty-four years later, in 1992, was won with a similar score of 278.
- The Scottish Professional Championship was won in 1960 with a score of 278.
- The winning score thirty-four years later: 281.

Things are no different with amateur golfers either. According to author Dr. Bob Rotella,

Fifteen years ago the average American male golfer's handicap was 16.2. The average female golfer's handicap was 29. Today, the average American male golfer's handicap is 16.2, and the average female golfer's handicap is 29!

A very interesting conclusion can be drawn from these facts: Golfers haven't improved despite technological advances!

Here is a short story: A baby elephant is conditioned by its captors to believe that it cannot escape when tied to a small stick in the ground. As the elephant grows up, its captors can keep it tethered to the same small stick, even though the fully-grown animal can easily pull a large tree out of the earth! Although correctly fitted, appropriate golf equipment is important, golfers, too, have always believed that to reach their potential, practice, lessons, and good clubs were all that were required. They have been tied to the belief that high-tech equipment and dedicated practice is all it takes to play the best golf.

Just as the grown elephant can release itself from captivity when it realizes the weakness of its restraint, so too can the golfer break away from previously learned behavior. Golfers

need to realize that golf is an athletic game and that they are athletes. Until golfers adopt an athletic attitude and conditioning for their sport, they will continue to suffer stagnation, as demonstrated by the virtually nonexistent improvement in golf scores over the past few decades.

Posture and the Golfing Athlete

What is posture? The word *posture* is commonly used among golf pros, yet, watching a tournament on TV, it will only take a few seconds to find a player with bad posture. Why do you suppose everyone is so mentally conscious of posture, yet not so physically aware of it?

Posture, like the size of your nose or the shape of your ear, is not something you can just think about and expect to change. However, like your weight or the size of your biceps, posture can be improved, and good posture is a skill that should be the foundation of golf conditioning. Fifty years ago, posture was on the forefront of osteopathic, chiropractic, physical therapy, and orthopedic studies. In fact, posture has been important to yogis for thousands of years. Why, then, has posture deteriorated drastically in our culture? Certainly obesity, sedentary lifestyles, and lack of awareness have played a role.

How Do We Define "Good Posture"?

One of my favorite definitions of posture is "the position from which movement begins and ends." This definition is particularly useful when you consider that a person's posture is a physical result of the interaction between the mind and body—nervous system and musculoskeletal system. If you begin and end movement with poor posture, you greatly increase the chance of joint wear and tear and injury.

Within the definition of posture, we must also look at different types of posture:

- *Static posture*, or stationary posture, is the position of the body at rest, sitting, standing, or lying.
- *Dynamic posture*, or moving posture, is the maintenance of what's called "the instantaneous axis of rotation of any/all working joints in any spatial or temporal relationship." In other words, your joints should always be lined up in their proper working positions during the full range of any given motion, specifically, the golf swing.

A good example of the difference between static and dynamic posture is commonly found in professional dancers. Prior to a performance, you will often see them sitting in a slouched posture while having their makeup applied, eating a snack, or talking to friends. The instant a dancer walks onto the dance floor, it is as if someone else now inhabits her body—her posture suddenly improves to near perfect standards, particularly when in motion.

This is an important point for golfers because sitting or standing in good postural alignment does not guarantee maintenance of the same posture the instant they address a golf ball and perform a full swing. The postural attitude in any given situation is part of the *engram*, or motor memory, of past experiences of the same task. It becomes evident from this discussion of static and dynamic posture that achieving a healthy postural awareness from both perspectives is necessary. Both the static and dynamic posture of the golfer are of equal importance and should be considered.

The Golf Swing from a Dynamic Posture Perspective

Which muscles and joints are involved in the golf swing? Well, a safe answer would be all of them. Next time you watch someone swing a golf club, take notice of how many joints are moving; practically every joint in the body works at some point during a golf swing, making it a very complex movement.

Every golfer wants a low handicap. A low handicapper must be consistent. To be consistent, you must be able to reproduce a good swing every time. To appreciate the neuromechanical challenge a golf swing places on the body, let's look at some of the basic biomechanical requirements.

Posture and Golf

Golf requires full rotational capacity of nearly every joint involved. Golf is a rotation sport; to reach your golf potential, you must be able to repeatedly rotate efficiently and explosively.

Consider a known physical principle: force applied to an object imparts to it an acceleration, not only in translation but also in rotation; the object turns around its own center of gravity. This is important, as rotation may cause the affected vertebrae to displace from the normal position; chiropractors and osteopaths refer to the misalignment of such vertebrae as *subluxation*.

Golfers with inadequate postural alignment, muscle imbalance syndromes, and associated joint motion restriction will not be able to rotate efficiently. This was proven by Moshe Feldenkrais who, in comparing humans and animals, calculated mathematically the moment of inertia of the body around the vertical axis.

Feldenkrais noted that when animals adopt a bipedal stance, the head leans forward and is balanced by the pelvis protruding backward. The result is that the moment of inertia around the vertical axis is four to five times greater than humanlike vertical alignment.

The position in which the pelvis, trunk, and head are aligned vertically and the spinal curvatures are at a minimum is the position in which minimum muscular contraction is necessary to keep the body from falling over. The smallest amount of muscular tone is consequently required in that posture. As the golfer deviates from ideal spinal alignment, muscular tone increases, as do energy requirements, causing performance to decrease and the incidence of musculoskeletal pain to increase.

Factors That Determine the Flight and Destination of a Ball

Virtually every PGA playing and teaching pro knows that ball flight is primarily controlled by five factors:

1. Club face alignment
2. Swing path
3. Angle of attack
4. Hitting the sweet spot
5. Clubhead speed

Swing faults are to be expected when a player's swing displays characteristics that adversely affect one or more of the above factors. A golf pro consulting with a player will typically identify the aspects of the swing that are producing aberrant ball flight and will then attempt to instruct the player on how to correct it. Frequently, adjustments will be made in stance, swing amplitude, hip/shoulder turn ratio, grip, and so on, until the player gets it right. However, in the majority of players, these swing changes are merely compensating for imbalances in the musculoskeletal structures of their bodies. These changes in the swing are merely a way of "tricking the system" and allow a player to overcome the swing fault of primary concern—for the time being.

The body is a complex system of interrelated systems. The systems predominantly involved in producing the swing are the nervous system, muscular system, and skeletal system; all combined, they create the neuromechanical system.

The player's neuromechanical system's state of readiness can always be determined by assessing the following four physical factors. These four factors all affect ball flight:

1. Muscle balance and flexibility
2. Static and dynamic postural stability
3. Strength
4. Power

Table 5.1 Correlating Ball-Flight Factors and Physical Factors

Ball-Flight Factors	Physical Factors
Clubface alignment (1, 2)	1. Muscle balance and flexibility
Swing path (1, 2)	2. Static and dynamic postural stability
Angle of attack (1, 2)	3. Strength
Hitting the sweet spot (1, 2)	4. Power
Clubhead speed (1, 2, 3, 4)	

Review Table 5.1 for a moment. In the left-hand column are the five factors that control ball flight. The numbers in parentheses next to each of the five ball flight factors indicate which of the four physical factors (right-hand column) impart the greatest influence on them. For example, the physical factors most affecting clubface alignment are muscle balance and flexibility and static and dynamic postural stability. In fact, if you look closely, those two physical factors are the deciding influence in *four of the five ball-flight factors!* In other words, golfers who are trying to hit the ball harder and faster would improve much more if they focused on muscle balance, flexibility, and postural stability. If physical factors 1 and 2 are not adequately addressed and attempts are not made to improve physical factors 3 and 4, you only get to walk further into the rough!

6

GOLF ANATOMY AND BIOMECHANICS

Golf is an athletic sport that is physically demanding and can lead to injury. The swing motion itself puts tremendous amounts of stress on the body. These demands are greater on the less-skilled player versus a professional or elite amateur. The general public has a misconception that golf is solely a technical sport with few physical demands. To completely understand the importance of improving the physical game, a golfer must have a basic understanding of golf's physical motion, or *biomechanics*. This chapter will outline the physical demands of the sport, giving you a better understanding of how the body moves.

The golf swing itself is one of the most studied movements in all of sports. Thousands of articles, books, and videos have been written on proper technique. In this chapter, we will specifically focus on the *body movement* required to complete a successful swing motion, leaving proper technique to the PGA teaching professional.

The golf swing has evolved greatly over the past decades. In the 1920s, players such as Bobby Jones used a large body turn with a tendency to turn their hips and shoulders the same amount during the swing motion. This swing method, known as the *classic golf swing*, produced a flatter swing plane with a more upright and relaxed finish.

In contrast, the *modern golf swing* uses a much steeper swing plane. This steep plane combined with a large or maximal shoulder turn and restricted lower-body movement creates a coiling effect throughout the spine. Coiling can be very powerful but also creates excessive stress, especially when not done properly. The modern player also tends to finish with the back more arched than upright. These differences typically make the modern golf swing more stressful to the body than the classic golf swing.

The Spine

If we look at the human backbone or spine, we see that the vertebrae sit or stack on top of one another, producing a flexible but strong supporting structure. The spine itself is divided into various regions. There are seven vertebrae in the neck (cervical), twelve vertebrae in the midback (thoracic), and five vertebrae in the lower back (lumbar). Beneath the lumbar segments are found the sacrum and coccyx. Each segment is held together by a series of ligaments and muscles that connect to the spine and give it support. For golfers, the spine serves as the flexible connection between the upper and lower body. Proper function of the spine is essential to allow the coiling and uncoiling needed to produce a powerful swing motion. The spine has a natural S-shape when we stand upright. It is this upright neutral position that must be maintained to protect the spine while playing golf.

The golf swing is a complicated dynamic movement that consists of a series of rotations and counter-rotations of the spine and extremities. A right-handed golfer will experience a full rotation to the right then back to the left during a modern golf swing. This motion even when done with flawless mechanics will produce a certain amount of bending, twisting, sliding, and compression through the spine. In addition, because the golf swing occurs so quickly, between .95 and 1.25 seconds, these stresses may be significantly increased leaving a potential for injury to almost any body part.

The golf swing, especially the modern golf swing, puts a tremendous amount of stress on the back, neck, and extremities.

Trunk and/or spine motion can basically occur in three different directions:

- Forward and backward bending
- Lateral or side bending
- Rotation toward the right and left

Due to the spine motion described above, a golfer will experience the following forces on the spine during a normal golf swing:

1. Shear: the sliding force between segments of the spine
2. Compression: the downward force between segments
3. Sidebending: the right or left bending force on the spine
4. Rotational torsion: the amount of twisting between the spine segments

Not all spine motions produce the same stress potential or can directly lead to injury. Golfers need to be aware of the potential stresses that exist from extreme positions and excessive movements often seen with improper technique.

There are many different swing methods and techniques that are used successfully in competition today, with many of these methods being authored and taught by the games top teaching professionals. It is important to note that all golf swings create stress on the body. It is the amount of force and risk of injury that will vary tremendously between golf swings.

Golf injuries are most often caused by the repetitive stress of practice and play. Few people could disagree that golf is stressful when during a typical round of golf the golfer:

- Walks approximately 4 to 5 miles
- Takes over 100 practice and actual swings
- Leans over 30 to 40 putts
- Bends down 40 to 50 times

Flexibility and/or joint restrictions can translate stress to vulnerable areas, such as the spine. Proper technique is essential to reduce stress during the golf swing. A golfer who encounters biomechanical problems with his or her swing motion may need swing technique changes under the guidance of a qualified PGA teaching professional.

The following is a description of normal anatomy and biomechanics during the golf swing. This information can be used as a guideline to identifying which parts of the body are most critical to a successful golf swing and should be addressed during a golf fitness or conditioning program.

Phases of the Golf Swing

The typical golf swing has five phases:

1. Address
2. Backswing
   a. Takeaway
   b. Top of the backswing
3. Downswing
4. Impact
5. Follow-through

Address

Definition: The position of your body just before initiating the golf swing.

When setting up to the ball, the upper body leans forward to bring the club head down to the ground. Ideally, the golfer should bend forward at the hips rather than at the spine. The spine should remain upright in a naturally tall posture, maintaining a slightly outward curved midback and slightly inward curved low back without excessive roundness in either position. This spine position combined with the natural relaxed position of the shoulders and arms is called the *neutral position*. By maintaining the neutral position throughout the golf swing, a golfer will protect his or her back and maximize flexibility. The further an athlete deviates from this neutral position, the greater the potential for stress.

The address position places stress on the body due to the forward bending of the trunk over the feet. As the balance point, or center of gravity, of the trunk shifts over the middle portion of the foot, it causes increased muscle activity of all the posterior, or backside muscles located in the hips, trunk, and neck. These extensor muscles are responsible for keeping us upright and balanced. Because of the stance position, at address, a slight increase in tension is noted in all the major thigh muscles. This muscle activity is in response to the anticipated movement of the arms that will occur during the next phase of the swing, the backswing.

Summary of Address Biomechanics

- Shoulders and arms are relaxed, in front of the body.
- Spine is in a relaxed neutral position.
- Slight side bend occurs at the spine due to the right hand being lower on the club.
- Hips and knees are slightly bent.

Summary of Muscle Activity

- Arms are in front of the body with tension in the forearms, wrists, and hands.
- Trunk and spine extensors, or back muscles, are stabilized to hold the address position.
- The major lower extremity muscles are also active and functioning to stabilize. These muscles include the quadriceps, or front of the thigh muscles, hip adductors, or groin, and the hip extensors, including the hamstrings and the calves.

Backswing

Definition: The process of moving the club head from the address position to the top of the arc of the swing.

Takeaway. The takeaway, or first part of the backswing, is not particularly stressful; the shoulders and trunk ideally rotate as one stable unit. The trunk and abdominal muscles are most responsible for controlling this movement. These muscle groups are used to control stress to the spine by providing stability from the top of the pelvis to the bottom of the ribs. The trunk stabilizers include the abdominal and the back muscles. These muscles tighten together to brace and protect this region of the body.

Top of the Backswing. As the club moves to the top of the backswing, a number of factors can lead to unnecessary stress. The path of the club directly dictates the direction of stress on the spine. In comparison, the classic swing used a relatively flat path or plane, while the modern swing uses a more upright plane. A steeper or more upright plane, consistent with the modern golf swing, causes more stress because the twisting of the upper body occurs vertically while the hips and lower spine twist in a more horizontal direction. This coiling in different directions generates power but can also cause injury.

Side bending of the trunk and spine is also not a very desirable motion during the golf swing. The amount of side bending seen is directly related to the amount of sliding that occurs at the hips as the golfer moves into the backswing. This excessive side-bending motion can cause a dipping of the left shoulder and head at the top of the backswing, leading to a common swing fault called a *reverse weight shift*, or pivot. Strong evidence exists that excessive side bending is extremely stressful to the low back.

At the top of the backswing, we typically see a difference in the amount of rotation between the turns at the shoulders and hips. For touring professionals, we often see a 45 degree hip turn and a 90 degree shoulder rotation. The difference between these motions is called the *X factor*. Although increasing your X factor has been shown to increase distance, golfers will see greater benefits from working on their flexibility through the spine rather than attempting to rotate their spine beyond its normal limits.

Summary of Backswing Biomechanics

Movement during this phase of the golf swing occurs as a dynamic sequence of events:

- The head rotates toward the left.
- Counter-rotation occurs at the shoulders, midback, and lumbar spine toward the right (approximately 90 degrees).
- Rotation of the lower extremities (approximately 45 degrees).
- The hips experience relative rotation toward the left as compared to the trunk above, allowing the golfer to maintain a stable base.
- The knees will maintain a slightly bent position.
- A weight shift occurs, causing the golfer to load the inner part of the right foot between the ball and heel.

Summary of Muscle Activity

As we have seen, the backswing is a complicated sequence of movements that occurs as the golfer rotates the trunk and lifts the club with the upper extremities.

- The shoulder muscles are active as the club moves away from the ball. The shoulder girdle remains active, including the rotator cuff, as the golfer lifts the club.
- The hand and wrist muscles all work to control the weight of the club as the club is positioned above the head at the top of the backswing.

- The oblique abdominals and the erector spinae, or spine extensors, work to rotate the trunk.
- The right hip internal rotators and left hip external rotators are active.

Downswing

Definition: The phase of the golf swing when the club is brought from the top of the backswing toward impact.

There are many different cues to initiate the downward motion of the golf swing. For some it is the hands, while others teach the hips or trunk. From an injury prevention standpoint, the golfer must properly link or transfer motion from one part of the body to the next. For golfers, a typical sequence will include transferring motion first from the lower body to the trunk or torso, then through the shoulders and hands, and finally to the club, maximizing speed at ball impact. It is essential for the abdominal groups to be active during this process, especially as a golfer moves the trunk. This will assure a stable posture for the back. Remember, if the spine is out of its neutral position it is vulnerable.

Summary of Downswing Biomechanics

- The transition at the top of the backswing occurs when the direction of swing changes from right to left. This begins the uncoiling phase of the golf swing. This phase is most stressful to the body if combined with poor technique.
- The highest forces of side bending, shear, and rotation occur at the neck and low back during this phase.
- The golfer must properly link the motion that occurs during this phase of the golf swing, allowing the efficient transfer of energy from one segment of the body to the next. The proper timing or linking of this motion will maximize club-head speed.

Impact

Definition: The phase of the golf swing where ball contact occurs.

It should not be surprising that the majority of the injuries occur during this phase of the golf swing when the most parts of the body are moving, maximum velocity is reached, and contact is made with the ball. The spine is most susceptible if the golfer slides toward the target. Depending on the magnitude and velocity of this slide, injury can occur. For golf, sliding stresses are generally considered the most dangerous. Controlling the amount of hip slide is crucial from a physical training standpoint.

Summary of Impact Biomechanics

At impact:

- The head and neck experience a side-bending motion toward the right, combined with a forward bend.
- Shoulders are now brought back to a square position.
- The midback and low back experience a side-bending motion toward the right combined with a rotational motion toward the left.
- The lower body is turning, with the hips being slightly open toward the target.

Summary of Muscle Activity

- The greatest muscle activity and tension is produced as the muscles contract to bring the club to the ball.
- The shoulder girdle, including the rotator cuff, is active. Other muscles, including the serratus anterior, which connects the shoulder blade to the rib cage, and the pectoral or chest muscles are actively accelerating the arms.
- The midback muscles, including the lower trapezius, act to stabilize the shoulder blade.

- The trunk muscles, including the abdominal groups and the erector spinae, or spine extensors, are active.
- The hip muscles that are most active include the hip rotators, hip adductors, and hip abductors. Hip-rotator weakness is common in golf. If the hip adductors and abductors are dominant during this phase, the golfer may lack leg stability and a sliding motion can occur.
- All leg muscles are active as weight is being transferred from the right to the left side.

Follow-Through

Definition: The phase of the golf swing past impact.

The follow-through, or finish, involves a full rotation of the body toward the target. Provided that this rotation occurs with the spine in a straight position, the finish is usually well tolerated and produces minimal stress. A follow-through position consisting of either excessive side bending or excessive arching of the spine (reverse C) can lead to pain or injury.

Summary of Follow-Through Biomechanics

This is the slowing down or decelerating phase of the golf swing.

- The pelvis and trunk have turned toward the target.
- The left hip rotates, straightens, and moves toward the midline of the body, while the right hip moves to a neutral position facing the target.
- The left knee straightens, while the right knee remains bent with balance on the toes.
- The spine maintains a neutral or slightly side-bent position toward the right.
- The shoulders move in reverse motion of the backswing, with the club finishing overhead.

Ideally, as the club moves through ball impact it is accelerating. Postimpact, the club will immediately begin to decelerate. The muscles that are active during this phase of the golf swing work together to provide two specific functions:

- Rotation of the body to a balanced finish position. The golfer needs to maintain support for approximately 95 percent of her body weight on the left leg as she finishes the golf swing. The ability to complete this activity requires strength and balance of the hip and trunk muscles.
- Deceleration of the body as the golf club is moved to a position over the left shoulder.

Strengthening Various Muscle Groups

All parts of the body can benefit from building strength, but golfers should key in on these specific areas:

- *The thighs.* Four different muscles on the front of the thigh collectively called the quadriceps help provide power during the forward swing and acceleration through the ball. The hamstrings, the muscles in the back of the thigh, initiate pelvic rotation and allow the transfer of power from the hips to the trunk and arms.
- *The hips and buttocks.* These muscles, especially the gluteus maximus, the largest in the buttocks, are most active during the forward swing, generating power.
- *Back muscles.* The back muscles have an important function related to proper golf posture. These muscles hold us up and help us maintain our address position. The back muscles are most active during the downswing, as we accelerate through impact. They also help to decelerate the body during the follow-through. The latissimus dorsi, a large back muscle, is critical in starting hip

movement. The latissimus dorsi also attaches to the upper arm, therefore aiding in arm rotation.

- *The abdominals.* These may be the most important golf muscles! These muscles not only aid in posture and balance but also help to brace and protect the spine. The deepest of the four abdominal muscles, the transverse abdominus muscle acts like a girdle to compress the abdominal viscera and stabilize the trunk. This function helps to protect the back from injury. The oblique abdominals are essential to properly rotate the trunk, providing power during the forward motion of the golf swing. The internal and external oblique muscles are located on the sides of the trunk below the rib cage. The rectus abdominus muscle helps each golfer maintain a forward bent posture through ball impact and therefore plays an active role in maximizing performance.
- *Chest.* The pectoral major is the largest chest muscle. This muscle pulls the arm down through the golf ball, providing power as the golfer moves toward the finish.
- *Shoulders.* The most important shoulder muscles used during the golf swing are the four rotator cuff muscles. These muscles work together to stabilize the shoulder, coordinate the swing, and protect the joint.
- *Forearm muscles.* These muscles lend control and touch during the swing, particularly during the short game.

7

DETERMINING YOUR BASELINE— WHERE TO START

*The score is important, of course. And the
discovery that you are superior to another golfer
is satisfying. But when your score is bad
and the other fellow beats you,
golf still has been a blessing to you.
The score isn't the "be all and end all."*
—TOMMY ARMOUR

Developing a clear intention and clear goals, for both the physical body and for golf performance, is essential for success. The purpose of the baseline evaluation is to establish a starting point for your physical condition. By developing this baseline, you will be able to chart your progress.

Baseline Rotational Test

Standing with feet hip-width apart, inhale, lifting the right arm to shoulder height. Revolve the torso clockwise and align the forefinger with a spot behind you (Figure 7.1). Repeat on the other side. Remember this mark so you can chart your progress.

Figure 7.1

Figure 7.2

Lower-Extremity Hip-Flexibility Testing

Place the club behind the shoulders and begin a deep knee squat (Figure 7.2). Do not let the knees go beyond 90 degrees past the knees. Pay attention to your ability to flex the hips.

Estimated angle of hip flexion: _____

Date: _____

Figure 7.3

Lower-Body Strength Testing

Standing (or with the back against the wall), walk the feet approximately two feet out. Maintain a 90-degree angle at the knee (Figure 7.3). Press the navel toward the spine, low back pressing against the wall. Hold for as many seconds as possible; chart the length of time.

Number of seconds or minutes: _____

Date: _____

Figure 7.4

Abdominal Strength

With the knees bent and feet flat on the floor, sit with the upper body upright. Cross the arms in front of the chest, slightly tucking in the chin. Slowly roll back until you feel the abdominals working and hold (Figure 7.4). Begin to count seconds until muscle fatigue.

Number of seconds: _____

Date: _____

Upper-Body Strength

On all fours, place the hands slightly in front of the shoulders. Bring the chest toward the floor, as if performing a modified push-up, elbows hugging the sides of the body (Figure 7.5). Repeat as many times as possible to muscle fatigue.

    Number of repetitions: _____

    Date: _____

Figure 7.5

Hamstring/Low-Back Flexibility

Sitting with legs wider than shoulder-width apart, reach forward with the hands stretched out, and mark the edges of the fingers on part of the leg (Figure 7.6).

    Fingers placed on the leg: _____

    Date: _____

Figure 7.6

Torso Flexibility

Lie on your back, knees bent, with the heels as close as possible to the buttocks. Arms are stretched out from the body, palms facing up. Gently let the knees fall to the left (Figure 7.7). Imagine half a clock face over the knees, from nine to three. Mark the number on the clock. Rotate to the other side and repeat.

    Clock number: _____

    Date: _____

Figure 7.7

    Having developed this baseline, you now can track your progress. If practicing Yoga for Golfers three times a week, retest in four weeks.

8

GUIDELINES AND STRATEGIES FOR A SUCCESSFUL YOGA EXPERIENCE

I figure practice puts brains in your muscles.
—SAM SNEAD

Following these guidelines will help you have a safe, effective, and fun yoga experience:

- Get written permission from your physician clearing you to participate in this or any other physical fitness program.
- Find a quiet place, free from interruptions and loud noises. The space should be warm to ensure that muscles remain flexible. If necessary, heat the room before beginning your yoga practice.
- Set goals and be realistic. If you only have fifteen minutes a day to practice, don't attempt to complete thirty poses. Adherence to the program is more important than completing as many poses as possible.
- Vary your yoga practice. A possibility is to work on varying body parts such as shoulders, low back, and core one day, and hips, wrists, and core another day.

- Yoga is best when practiced on an empty or almost empty stomach. A piece of fruit or glass of juice is acceptable, but not a stack of pancakes.

- You should never experience pain in the muscles, joints, or nerves. Slight discomfort as the muscle is stretching is acceptable, but pain is not. Be gentle and patient— Rome wasn't built in a day.

- Always modify poses if necessary, paying keen attention to the body and its reaction to each pose.

- It is more beneficial to hold the poses for an extended period of time than to move in and out of the poses quickly.

- Never bounce in a pose. Move into the pose as deeply as possible and hold that position, creating a static posture. Bouncing or ballistic stretching can cause injury to the muscle.

- Remember to flex the opposing muscle. This will create a stretch reflex in the antagonist muscle, sending the message for the muscle to relax. For example, it is necessary to squeeze, flex, or engage the quadriceps when attempting to stretch the hamstring.

- It is always helpful to keep the core slightly engaged; in other words, gently draw the navel toward the spine at all times. This facilitates support of the lumbar spine. In addition, lifting the rib cage off the waist supports better posture and increases diaphragmatic breathing capacity.

- Individuals with high blood pressure and glaucoma should keep the head above the heart.

- Those with hip replacements should keep the femur to the outside of the navel. Those with knee replacements should maintain a 90 degree or greater angle of knee flexion. Get written permission from your doctor before you begin.

- Do not overstretch areas that are already flexible. Functional strength in the joint is equally as important as flexibility. One can become too flexible.

- Make the commitment to become curious about your yoga practice and your golf game. Read and reread the biomechanical section in this book to learn more about your body. Research the many books available on the mental side of the game.

- Keep a positive attitude and realize that the body responds very quickly to yoga practice. And remember, you are never too old to begin yoga.
- Have fun and enjoy the process!

Finding More Joy

A sports psychologist friend of mine specializes in the study of peak performance for athletes, executives, and individuals. Through his past research, he uncovered a consistent characteristic linked to elite performance—enjoyment of the sport. Enjoyment or joy is defined as happiness, fulfillment, acceptance, tolerance, and mindfulness.

As part of his master's thesis, my friend spent two weeks sitting just off the eighteenth hole of a golf course in Arizona. He queried each of the golfers as they finished with one simple question, "How was your round?" As you can imagine, the answers varied drastically. From responses of sheer happiness at hitting the ball so far it landed in the water to frustration at missing par by one stroke, my friend came to a number of conclusions. The younger the golfer, the more they experienced some form of joy such as finally getting to see a big snake on the seventh green, or hitting the ball into a cactus, or laughing out loud when one of their buddies "doffed" the ball. On the other hand, the older the golfer, the more criticism and frustration dominated their rounds. They complained of slow play, physical injuries, and the bad lies that caused the double bogies.

Watch most golfers walk from shot to shot: head down, deep in self-abusive thoughts, mentally scrambling for the perfect biomechanical tip to fix the current swing flaw. Where is the joy? Next time you are on the golf course, create a conscious shift in your thinking, from struggle to joy. Lift your head, capture the scenery (what is more beautiful than a golf course?), and breathe in the fresh air. Remember what you love about golf and make that your mantra.

Your internal dialogue has a direct effect on the external outcome. Shifting your thinking to thoughts of joy will facilitate a better outcome. You will experience a greater sense of fulfillment and harmony.

9

BREATHING AWARENESS—IN YOGA AND YOUR GOLF SWING

*Basketball is a complex dance that requires shifting
from one object to another at lightning speeds.
The secret is not thinking. That doesn't mean being stupid;
it means quieting the endless jabbering of thoughts
so that your body can do instinctively what it's been
trained to do without the mind
getting in the way.*
—PHIL JACKSON

The Sanskrit word for yoga breathing exercises is *prana-yama*. *Prana* refers to the energy in the body or life force, the fuel or oxygen that keeps us alive. *Yama* refers to expansion and extension, meaning the ability to expand the breath and increase the energy in the body. It is critical in golf to be aware of how the body and mind react to the stresses of the game. With awareness comes change!

Any time we experience stress on the golf course—during the first shot, a tight lie, or any shot that creates anxiety—our breathing becomes erratic. Physically, breathing sustains the body's metabolic processes; mentally, breathing keeps the mind calm and focused. When the body is relaxed, the lungs, the diaphragm, and the muscles of the rib cage and chest move in an unrestricted way. This is often referred to as deep diaphragmatic breathing. When under pressure, the physiological effect of holding the breath is a "fight-or-flight" response, resulting in rapid uncontrolled breathing and a loss of blood flow to the extremities, including the brain. The body becomes tense, the mind races, and the ability to execute the golf swing becomes more challenging. (As if we need more challenge!)

Your breathing pattern is a direct reflection of the level of stress on the body and mind at any given point. It is the mirror of your internal physical and mental condition.

Peter Kostis, commentator for CBS Sports and the USA Network, remarked on the stress level of Annika Sorenstam as she played on the PGA Tour (the first woman to play in fifty-three years). Discussing how to calm the swirl of emotions under these stressful situations, Peter said, "Annika has been able to control the heartbeat and control the emotions." There is only one way to calm the heartbeat and that is with the breath.

The most important aspect of yoga is the breath. Without focus on breathing, yoga is just another form of stretching. Here we address breathing awareness and how deep diaphragmatic and thoracodiaphragmatic breathing are used in yoga and on the golf course. Breathing awareness provides insight into the tempo and rhythm of your golf swing. According to Ernest Jones, "When you stroke with timing and rhythm, the ball sails straight down the fairway, and for distance. It is effortless power, not powerful effort."

We think of breathing as an automatic response and part of the automatic nervous system—it just happens. But at the same time, it is the only automatic response mechanism we can control. In the same way we manage movement, as in the golf swing or yoga postures, the breath is managed—its function originates in the two lowest segments of the brain stem. Also a function of the *somatic* nervous system, breathing can be controlled. This is what makes diaphragmatic movement so unique. Breathing relieves tension, and tension is the number-one cause of bad shots on the golf course.

Breathing consists of three basic components: inhalation, exhalation, and retention. Although retention can be an important part of expanding breathing and stimulating the nervous system, for our purposes we will focus on the inhales and exhales. In our dynamic or flow-yoga sequencing, the inhalations raise the body and the exhalations lower the body. Breathing influences movement in the abdomen and chest but also has an effect on posture.

To begin to understand the process, lie on your stomach, face pointed toward the floor (place a folded blanket or small pillow under your lower abdomen if you have low-back problems). Relax. Begin to inhale through the nose, and you will feel the body rise or lift. Exhale through the nose, and feel the body lower or fall. Before beginning a warm-up sequence of yoga poses intended to increase your breathing capacity, practice these simple deep diaphragmatic breathing techniques. Begin by lying on your back, knees bent, feet flat on the floor. Gently place your fingertips on your lower ribs. Close your eyes and begin to inhale and exhale as deeply as possible. Feel the movement in your fingers, reflecting the movement of the diaphragm. Begin by inhaling and exhaling for a count of four. If possible, increase the exhalation count to six. (Do not hold your breath at any point.)

Level 1: Ten breaths
Level 2: Twenty breaths
Level 3: Three minutes

Stretching the diaphragm, thoracic spine, and intercostals will open this part of the body, allowing the rib cage to expand and contract fully with each breath. See Chapter 28 for a series of poses designed to increase breathing capacity.

Golfers may incorporate this new breathing awareness into their preshot routine—calming the mind, facilitating greater focus, and developing more tempo in their swing.

To get a sense of "feeling" the tempo and rhythm in the swing, simply swing the club as if it were timed with a metronome. Coordinate your breathing with your swing tempo. Get a sense of ease and freedom in your swing.

For higher-handicap golfers, start by setting your golf stance completely and begin a long, slow, deep cleansing breath. Then begin your takeaway.

Paul Trittler, one of *Golf Magazine's* top 100 instructors, suggests the following preshot routine for lower-handicap golfers.

As you stand behind the ball, visualizing the ball flight, incorporate long, slow, deep breathing. As you sole the club, aim the face, set your back foot, and begin a deep inhalation. Then set your front foot, let your eyes go to the target, and begin to exhale. Once you have finished feeling your balance and completed your exhale, let your eyes go to the ball and swing.

10

VARIOUS FORMS OF YOGA

Above all, tempo is the great equalizer.
It compensates for mechanical flaws in your swing
and will reduce your slices, hooks,
and inconsistent contact.
—BILL MORETTI

The *Yoga for Golfers* program offers various levels of intensity, accommodating many fitness levels. In the dynamic or flow-yoga sequence of poses, you move rapidly from one pose to another. This style is considered more advanced and physically active. *Tapas* is the Sanskrit term referring to the heat and energy that is generated by physical movement and a sharp, focused mind.

In *flow yoga*, the muscles and cardiovascular systems are activated, saturating the body with blood flow. This system of yoga increases oxygen uptake and all the available nutrients to support greater flexibility and strength. Flow-yoga poses are held for one to five breaths. When the breath and physical movement coordinate, the cardiovascular system is engaged, and strength and endurance are increased.

The best examples of dynamic or flow yoga are Sun Salutations, a sequence of poses that are completed five times to warm the body and lubricate the muscles and joints. Each inhalation and exhalation represents one movement in the Sun Salutation.

Fluidity is the key here—please, no bouncing. As you move in and out of the pose, pay keen attention to your physical form. Flailing or bouncing the body in and out of each pose is not acceptable and can lead to injury. Move easily with the breath, aware of and accepting your current level of fitness. Your body will respond positively and quickly.

Static yoga is characterized by holding the poses for an extended number of breaths with a short break between poses. You move deeper into the pose, which brings tremendous benefits to the body as well as serenity to the mind. This style offers the opportunity to pay attention to proper alignment, and although it is considered to be less cardiovascular than flow yoga, you will experience an increased level of strength and flexibility.

Restorative yoga uses props such as blocks, straps, blankets, and bolsters to support the body in specific poses. These poses are held for minutes, sometimes as long as ten minutes, while the yogi rests, allowing gravity to do the work. Restorative yoga is intended to restore the body to its original level of health and well-being. *Yoga for Golfers* uses restorative yoga poses as a postround yoga practice. You will feel energized and rested and at the same time reduce your risk of injury and decrease your recovery time.

11

HOW TO
USE THIS BOOK

There are many ways to use this book. If you are challenged in a specific area of the body, practice the sequence designed for that area. There are yoga sequences based on time, ranging from fifteen to forty-five minutes. Adherence to a regular yoga practice is more important than the duration or length of time you practice. Be realistic about the time you have available to practice yoga and make the commitment. I recommend practicing a minimum of three days a week; four to five is optimum. Always practice the warm-up sequence before you play golf.

Always Remember M.B.A.—
The Three "Rules" of Practicing Yoga

- *Move slowly.* It is important to move in and out of the poses slowly with conscious awareness. This practice will reduce the risk of injury and enhance your ability to concentrate and remain focused.
- *Breathe deeply.* There should be no strain in the breathing, as it is a reflection of the intensity of the pose and agitation in the mind. Slow, deep breathing is the most important part of the yoga practice. In traditional stretching programs, the length of time a stretch should be held

varies. In yoga, we suggest you hold the poses for five to ten breaths. Please honor and respect your current physical condition by being aware of your breathing pattern. If the pose feels too elementary, move deeper into the pose, increasing the level of intensity while still maintaining even breathing.

- *Align the body carefully.* Pay close attention to proper body alignment. Just as in the golf stance, in yoga we begin by placing the feet firmly in the correct position and adjusting the body from the feet upward. There is greater value in keeping proper body alignment and moving half the distance in the pose than in improper alignment for a longer duration.

Using the baseline you determined in Chapter 7, you will establish the level of yoga that is most appropriate for your level of fitness.

- *Par Level.* The par series of poses represents a basic level yoga practice and offers modifications for more challenging poses. If you struggle with inflexibility, begin in the par series of poses.
- *Birdie Level.* The birdie series is slightly more advanced and a good level of intensity for the yoga practitioner or golfer who has a moderate amount of flexibility and fitness.
- *Eagle Level.* The eagle series is for the more advanced, physically fit golfer.

Important Terms

The following terms or instructions are ones that will be repeated in many of the poses, so it is important that you understand what is meant.

- *Moving to the edge of the pose.* As we have stated, one should not move so deeply into the pose as to cause pain.

You will feel the muscles working, sometimes to fatigue. Go to your edge, as far as is acceptable for you on that day, and hold the pose. Remember that every day is different. That is why we refer to the "yoga practice," not the "yoga perfect practice." The breathing should remain smooth and even, following your natural deep rhythm.

- *Drawing the navel toward the spine.* In almost every yoga posture, we work on the core strength of the abdominals. Lightly draw the navel inward, with slight effort, without gripping the abdominals too tightly.

- *Engaging the muscles.* Muscles are engaged or flexed to support relaxation of the antagonist or opposing muscles. A good example of this is the quadriceps and hamstring relationship. Flexing the quads sends a message to the hamstring to relax.

- *Tailbone down.* This phrase refers to pressing the tailbone down toward the floor. Engage the buttocks and then press the tailbone down. This action helps protect the lumbar spine in many of the core/back-strengthening poses.

- *"Telescoping the rib cage.* Often we refer to "lifting or telescoping the rib cage" of the waist. This exercise is a key component to working the core of the body, specifically the abdominals and back muscles. Inhale as you draw the navel inward, and then exhale, lifting the rib cage "off" the waist.

- *Sit bones.* This phrase refers to the bones at the top of the femurs that connect to the pelvis, sometimes referred to as the lowest part of the buttocks.

- *Bogies.* The "bogey" tips remind you of important aspects of the pose. Remember that proper alignment cannot be overemphasized.

Selecting the Right Series of Yoga for Golfers Poses for You

It is important to choose the right series of poses depending on your level of fitness or physical limitations.

- *Specific areas of the body.* For example, if you are challenged by low-back pain or want to increase your low-back strength and distance off the tee, go to the low-back section of the book and focus on that specific area.
- *Preround sequencing.* We provide sequencing of poses to be practiced at home, in the locker room, or on the golf course before the first tee. Taking ten minutes to prepare the body for the impact of the golf swing is essential.
- *Midround sequencing.* It is important to keep the muscles loose during the round. Stretching the shoulders and back every three holes will keep your swing fluid (demonstrated in Chapter 31, "On the Golf Course."
- *Postround sequencing.* Sports and exercise physiologists agree on the critical importance of postgame stretching. If you do not have the time directly after the round, practice our postround sequence designed for the home.

12

THE WARM-UP SEQUENCE

Do not use your body to move the club. Let your body respond to the moving of the club.
—Jim Flick

Warming up for your yoga practice is as important as warming up for golf. Just as the mind needs time to decompress and become more relaxed and focused, the body needs time to generate blood flow to the muscles. Be moderate in the intensity of the poses. These sequences can be done as preyoga or pregolf preparation and require approximately five to ten minutes.

Par Sequence
(Figures 12.1–12.6)

Figure 12.1 Cat/cow pose (cat position)

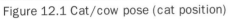

Figure 12.2 Cat/cow pose (cow position)

Figure 12.3 Downward-facing puppy

Figure 12.4 Twisting table pose

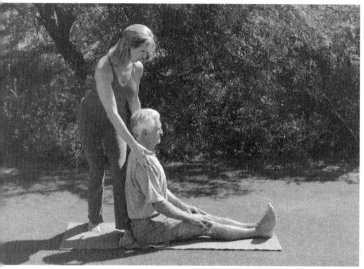

Figure 12.5 Staff pose (with back against the wall)

Figure 12.6 Bound-angle pose (with back against the wall)

Figure 12.7 Cat/cow pose (cat position)

Figure 12.8 Cat/cow pose (cow position)

Figure 12.9 Downward-facing dog

Birdie Sequence
(Figures 12.7–12.12)

Figure 12.10 Locust pose with one arm extended at a time

Figure 12.11 Cobra with block pose

Figure 12.12 Lying-down extended hand-to-foot twist

13

SUN SALUTATIONS

The Sun Salutation sequence warms up the body by generating increased blood flow to the muscles. This sequence requires special attention to breathing. Inhale as the body rises, while lifting the arms over the head, and exhale as the body folds forward. Focus on creating a sense of rhythm and tempo in the Sun Salutations, as the breathing is coordinated with each movement, just as in the golf swing.

Par and Birdie Sequence

After the warm-up sequence practice, do these three Sun Salutations before your full yoga practice.

- Standing pose: Standing with feet together, arms by your side, engage the quadriceps (Figure 13.1).

Figure 13.1

- Raised standing pose: Inhale, bringing the arms over the head (Figure 13.2).

Figure 13.2

- Forward fold: Exhale as you fold forward. Keep the knees slightly bent if necessary (Figure 13.3).

Figure 13.3

Figure 13.4

- Half-forward fold: Inhale as you slide the hands with the arms straight up to the shins or knees. Lengthen the spine, drawing the shoulders back, eyes focused in front of the mat. Keep the back of the neck long; avoid scrunching the neck (Figure 13.4).

Figure 13.5

- Crescent-lunge pose: Exhale, stepping the right foot back. Come high onto the fingertips, drawing the shoulders back, chest forward, eyes focused toward the front of the mat (Figure 13.5).

Figure 13.6

- Three-pointed push-up pose: Exhale, bringing the chin and chest toward the floor. Elbows hug the sides of the body; do not let them flare out to the sides. Draw the navel toward the spine, keeping the back flat and supporting the core (Figure 13.6).

Figure 13.7

- Modified cobra pose: Inhale, bringing the body to the
  floor, hands placed under the shoulders. Exhale.
  Spread fingers wide keeping the palms flat. On the next
  inhalation, draw the navel inward, engage the legs
  and buttocks. Lift the chest, shoulders back, while the
  pubic bone remains on the floor (Figure 13.7).

Figure 13.8

- Downward-facing dog: Exhale, lifting the hips from your
  core, and press back into the pose, keeping the knees bent
  as necessary. Feel as if you are pressing the mat toward
  the front of the room. Activate the quads while moving
  the weight into the legs. (Figure 13.8).

Figure 13.9

- Crescent-lunge pose: Inhale, stepping the right foot forward into a lunge position. The knee angle should not be more than 90 degrees (Figure 13.9).

- Forward fold: Exhale, stepping the left foot up to meet the right, and fold forward (Figure 13.10).

Figure 13.10

- Raised standing pose: Inhale, raising the arms over the head (Figure 13.11).

Figure 13.11

• Standing pose: Exhale, bringing the arms down by your sides (Figure 13.12).

Figure 13.12

Eagle Sequence

After the warm-up sequence, practice three Sun Salutations before your full yoga practice.

• Standing pose: Standing with feet together, arms by your side, engage the quadriceps (Figure 13.13). Feel yourself becoming very grounded, connected to the earth. Lift the toes, spread them wide, and gently relax the toes. From the waist down you become "rooted," growing tall from the waist up.

Figure 13.13

- Raised standing pose: Inhale as you bring the arms over the head (Figure 13.14).

Figure 13.14

- Forward fold: Exhale as you "swan dive" the body forward. Keep the knees slightly bent (Figure 13.15).

- Half-forward fold: Inhale, sliding the hands with the arms straight up to the shins or knees. Lengthen the spine, drawing the shoulders back, eyes focused in front of the mat. Keep the back of the neck long; avoid scrunching the neck. Envision the strength of the core as you lengthen from the hips to the head. Keep the weight evenly distributed over the feet, not the heels (Figure 13.16).

Figure 13.16

Figure 13.15

Figure 13.17

- Crescent-lunge pose: Exhale, stepping the right foot back. Come high onto the fingertips, drawing the shoulders back, chest forward, eyes focused toward the front of the mat (Figure 13.17). Engage the right leg, heel pressing away from you.

Figure 13.18

- Plank pose: Inhale, bringing the body to a plank position. Draw the navel inward, supporting the low back. Bring the inner ankles and inner thighs together, engaging the buttocks (Figure 13.18).

Bogey: Do not allow the low back to sink. Use the core strength to support the plank.

Figure 13.19

- Push-up pose: Exhale, lowering the body to three to four inches off the ground. Elbows hug the sides of the body; do not let them flare out to the sides (Figure 13.19). Maintain a parallel position of the upper arm. Do not drop the shoulders down.

Figure 13.20

- Upward-facing dog: Inhale, rolling on the toes as you bring the body forward. Keep the legs off the floor as you roll forward onto the tops of the feet. Press both hands into the floor as the thighs lift off the floor, chest forward and shoulders back. Engage the buttocks to protect the low back. Be sure you lift out of the shoulders and avoid sinking into this pose (Figure 13.20). Remember to draw the navel in, tailbone down, rib cage up.

Figure 13.21

- Downward-facing dog: Exhale, lifting the hips from the core and press back into the pose (Figure 13.21). Press the heels toward the floor. Toes point slightly inward. Engage the quads.

Figure 13.22

- Crescent-lunge pose: Inhale, stepping the right foot forward into a lunge position. The knee angle should not be more than 90 degrees (Figure 13.22).

Figure 13.23

- Forward fold: Exhale, stepping the left foot up to meet the right, and fold forward (Figure 13.23). Allow the neck to relax.

- Raised standing pose: Inhale, raising the arms over the head (Figure 13.24).
- Standing pose: Exhale, bringing the arms down by your sides (Figure 13.25).

Figure 13.24   Figure 13.25

14

NECK AND TRAPEZIUS

Pressure is when you've got thirty-five bucks riding on a four-foot putt and you've only got five dollars in your pocket.
—LEE TREVINO

General Pose Information: So often we carry everyday life pressures in the neck and upper shoulders. Sitting at a computer, cradling the telephone, and poor posture all contribute to having a "pain in the neck."

Benefits

- Supports the body's ability to maintain proper head position during the backswing phase
- Reduces problem of the forward head position

Bogey: Be gentle when working the neck area. It is important to move slowly and never pull or crank on the neck. Shoulders should remain down, moving away from the ears.

Par How-To

Par #1: Ear to Right Shoulder

While standing, slowly press your right ear toward the right shoulder. Keep the face pointing forward (Figure 14.1). Hold for three breaths and switch sides.

Figure 14.1

Par #2: Rotation with Hand on Jaw

Turn the face and chin toward the right shoulder. Use the hand for additional resistance (Figure 14.2). Hold for three breaths and switch sides.

Figure 14.2

Birdie How-To

Birdie #1: Pressing Left Arm Down

While pressing the right ear toward the right shoulder, inhale and engage the left arm, then exhale and press the arm down toward the floor (Figure 14.3). This will create more resistance and intensity in the pose. Hold for five breaths and switch sides.

Figure 14.3

Figure 14.4

Birdie #2

Sitting on a blanket, lean to the right side and let the right ear move toward the shoulder while slightly looking down toward the right hand. Inhale, bringing the left arm up to shoulder height, then exhale while pressing the arm away from the body (Figure 14.4). Hold for five breaths and switch sides.

Eagle How-To

Eagle #1

Lift left arm and slowly move the arm down toward the floor, creating more resistance in the left side of the neck and trapezius (Figure 14.5). Hold for five breaths and switch sides. Move very slowly coming out of this pose.

Figure 14.5

Eagle #2

The right arm is lifted to a 90-degree angle at the armpit and elbow. The left arm sweeps under with palms touching, thumbs near the face (Figure 14.6).

Modification: Bring elbows and palms together. Inhale; exhale as elbows and hands move away from the body and face. Shoulders remain down as elbows lift upward. Hold for five breaths and switch sides.

Figure 14.6

15

HANDS AND WRISTS

Good golf is when the quality of the bad shots
equals the quality of the good shots.
—PETER KOSTIS

General Pose Information: As the aging process occurs, the first signs of arthritis (pain and stiffness) become evident in the joints of the fingers and in the wrists. Maintaining flexibility as well as strength in the hands and wrists reduces your risk of injury. This is your only connection to the club!

Benefits

- Supports hand, wrist, and forearm placement at the address position
- Provides greater club control supporting the "cocking and uncocking" wrist action in the swing
- Controls hand action throughout the swing
- Provides more feel and touch, particularly in the short game and putting

Begin by warming up the wrists by gently swinging the golf club, focusing on the wrist action. Do not bring the club face higher than your waist.

Tip: Keep a tennis ball near you. Squeeze and release tension on the ball. Repeat fifteen times.

Par How-To

Par #1: Extension and Flexion with Opposite Hand

Extend the right arm with palm facing away from you. Bring the left hand to the right palm or fingers. Increase the intensity by pressing the palm into the fingers (Figure 15.1). Hold for five deep breaths and switch sides. Turn the right palm toward you, the back of the hand facing away. Place the left hand on the back of the right hand, creating resistance in the wrist (Figure 15.2). Hold for five breaths and switch sides.

Figure 15.1

Figure 15.2

Par #2: Flexion and Extension Pressing into the Floor

Spread the fingers as wide apart as possible. Focus on pressing the base of the forefinger into the floor. Hold for five breaths (Figure 15.3). Press the back of the hand into the floor, spreading the fingers wide. Hold for five breaths (Figure 15.4).

Figure 15.3

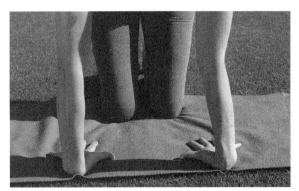

Figure 15.4

16

SHOULDERS

A golfer who learns to swing hard initially can
usually acquire accuracy later, whereas a golfer
who gets too accuracy conscious at the outset will rarely
be able to make himself hit the ball hard later on.
—JACK NICKLAUS

General Pose Information: Second to low-back injuries in golf are shoulder problems. Working the shoulders also supports increased shoulder strength through a full range of motion and better posture in the golf swing. These poses develop better postural alignment from rounded shoulders (a sign of bad posture) to shoulders back and chest forward.

Benefits

- Improves shoulder turn in the backswing
- Increases club control at adddress and top of the backswing
- Supports better posture at address and throughout the entire swing

Par How-To

Par #1: Shoulder Shrugs

Inhale, shrugging shoulders up toward the ears (Figure 16.1). Exhale, bringing shoulder blades together, and move shoulder blades down the back (Figure 16.2). This lifting and external rotation of the shoulder girdle will help with proper posture and shoulder rotation. Practice slowly for five repetitions.

Par #2: Downward-Facing Puppy

Begin on all fours, placing hands on the top of the mat. Spread the fingers with the palms flat. Inhale as the shoulders move away from the ears. Forearms remain off the mat (Figure 16.3). Exhale and begin to move buttocks toward the back of the mat. Note: Buttocks should not touch the heels, and a 90-degree angle should be maintained at the knee joint.

Bogey: Keep shoulders moving away from the ears, and no scrunching in the trapezius area. Keep the base of the forefingers pressing into the mat. This point in the hands provides a direct relationship to the shoulders.

Figure 16.1

Figure 16.2

Figure 16.3

Birdie How-To

Birdie #1: "Bird Wings"
Rotator-Cuff Exercise

Place elbows at a 90-degree angle, palms facing up. Elbows must hug the waistline. Inhale and externally rotate arms. Squeeze elbows into the waistline and hold (Figure 16.4). Exhale, returning to neutral position. Repeat five times.

Bogey: Keep the elbows pinned against the waistline. Allowing the elbows to flare out reduces the intensity of the pose.

Figure 16.4

Birdie #2:
Eagle Arms

The right arm is lifted to a 90-degree angle at the armpit and elbow.

Figure 16.5

The left arm sweeps under with palms touching and thumbs touching the face (Figure 16.5).

Modification: Bring elbows and hands together. Inhale; exhale while elbows and hands move away from the face. Shoulders are down as elbows lift upward. Hold for five breaths and switch sides.

Birdie #3: Standing Downward Dog with Hands on Club

Place hands on the top of the club. Step feet out wider than shoulder-width apart and create a 90-degree angle from the body to the legs. Draw the navel in and do not arch the back. Roll shoulders apart, moving the shoulders away from the ears (Figure 16.6). Hold for five breaths.

Bogey: Once in the pose, press hands into the club, pushing the sit bones toward the middle of the room. Engage the quadriceps, enhancing the stretch reflex to the hamstrings. Feel the adductors (inner thighs) squeezing toward the center of the body. Activate the feet by spreading the toes wide and lift in the arches.

Figure 16.6

Eagle How-To

Eagle #1: Downward-Facing Dog

Beginning on all fours, fingers spread wide, walk hands toward front of the mat. Slowly lift the hips, shifting the weight into the legs, pressing the spine long, pushing the mat away from you. Straighten the legs, heels moving toward the floor (Figure 16.7). Note: If hamstrings are very tight, it is acceptable to slightly bend the knees.

Bogey: The heels will eventually move toward the floor as hip and ankle flexion improve. Do not shorten the distance between the hands and feet to get the heels down. Envision the shape of a pyramid as the optimum position.

Figure 16.7

Eagle #2: Revolving Side-Angle Pose

Step the right foot forward as in the crescent-lunge position. You may modify the pose by lowering the left knee to the floor. Bring the left elbow to the outside of the right knee. Placing your hands into a "ball and socket" configuration, lift out of your left shoulder. Your left ear moves away from the shoulder. Eyes focus toward the floor or the ceiling (Figure 16.8). Do not strain the neck. Hold for seven breaths and switch sides.

Figure 16.8

17

RHOMBOIDS AND UPPER BACK

When you play golf, just play golf.
Here's you, here's the ball, there's the target.
Go for it. Hit the ball to the target as best you can.
Find the ball and do it again. Experience, adjust,
experience, adjust. . . . The golf course is made for
playing a game! So go there and play golf.
—CHUCK HOGAN

General Pose Information: The rhomboids (muscles of the upper back) help support the scapulae and posture. Stretching the upper back supports the shoulder turn.

Benefits

- Improves shoulder turn and stabilizes shoulder blades
- Increases club control and accelerates the arms at impact
- Reduces risk of rotator-cuff injury
- Supports better posture
- Alleviates upper-back pain
- Increases breathing capacity

Par How-To

Par #1: Rhomboid Stretch

Figure 17.1

Place your feet slightly wider than shoulder-width apart. Bend the knees and draw the navel toward the spine, supporting the back (Figure 17.1). Inhale, lacing hands together in front of body, and drop arms slightly lower than shoulder height. Exhale, pressing hands and arms away from the upper body. Feel the stretch in the upper back. Increase intensity by tucking the chin toward the chest. Hold for ten breaths.

Birdie How-To

Birdie #1: Downward Dog with a Chair

Place hands on the chair, shoulder-width apart. Step feet back to create a 90-degree angle from the body to the legs. Roll shoulders apart, moving the shoulders away from the ears. Press the hands into the chair, adding intensity to the shoulder stretch (Figure 17.2). Flex quads to increase the hamstring stretch. Hold for five to ten breaths.

Figure 17.2

Birdie #2: Twisting with Golf Club on Shoulders

Standing with feet wider than hip-width apart (simulating the golf stance), tilt at the hips, placing the golf club directly behind the shoulder blades. Inhale, drawing the navel in; telescope the rib cage up, and inhale deeply. Exhale, twisting the left shoulder toward the right side, looking over the right shoulder (Figure 17.3). Hold on the right side for five to ten breaths. Visualize the desired rotation in your back swing. Slowly release out of the pose, move to the other side and hold for five to ten breaths. Visualize the perfect finish position.

Figure 17.3

Bogey: Pay attention to maintaining the hip and spine angle throughout the pose. Maintain a solid right-leg position. This pose mimics the golf swing so it is important to not practice bad habits.

Eagle How-To

Eagle #1: Downward-Facing Dog

Beginning on all fours, fingers spread wide, walk hands toward front of the mat. Slowly lift the hips, shifting the weight into the legs, pressing the spine long, pushing the mat away from you. Straighten the legs, heels moving toward the floor (Figure 17.4). Note: If hamstrings are very tight, it is acceptable to slightly bend the knees.

Figure 17.4

Bogey: The heels will eventually move toward the floor, but do not shorten the distance between the hands and feet to get the heels down. Envision the shape of a pyramid as the optimum position.

Eagle #2: Eagle Arms

The right arm is lifted to a 90-degree angle at the armpit and elbow. The left arm sweeps under with palms touching and thumbs touching the face. Inhale; exhale with elbows and hands moving away from the face. Keep the shoulders down; only the elbows and hands lift upward (Figure 17.5). To modify the pose, bring the elbows and hands together.

Figure 17.5

18

ARMS

Benefits

- Provides club control during the take-away phase of the swing.
- Improves club head speed
- Strong arms control the weight of the club at the top of the swing

Par How-To

Par #1: Half-Cow Pose, Arms with Golf Club

Standing with feet wider than shouder-width apart or sitting, place a club in the right hand. Lift the arm up, palm facing the face, then allow the right hand to drop toward the back. Reach around the back and with the left arm grab onto the club (Figure 18.1). Hold this pose for five breaths; then switch sides and repeat.

Figure 18.1

Par #2: On All Fours, Three-Point Push-Ups

On all fours, hands placed slightly in front of the shoulders, drawing the navel in, slowly lower the chin and chest toward the floor (Figure 18.2). Keep arms hugging the sides of the body. Exhale on the exertion.

Figure 18.2

Modification: As you build strength, it is acceptable to lower the upper body only one to three inches.

Bogey: This pose specifically works the triceps and forearms. The elbows must hug the sides of the body—do not allow elbows to flare out.

Birdie How-To

Birdie #1: Downward-Facing Dog

Beginning on all fours, fingers spread wide, walk hands toward the front of the mat. Slowly lift the hips, shifting the weight into the legs, pressing the spine long, pushing the mat away from you. Straighten the legs, heels moving toward the floor (Figure 18.3). Note: If hamstrings are very tight, it is acceptable to slightly bend the knees.

Figure 18.3

Bogey: The heels will eventually move toward the floor, but do not shorten the distance between the hands and feet to get the heels down. Envision the shape of a pyramid as the optimum position.

Eagle How-To
Eagle #1: Plank-Pose Push-Ups

Placing the hands directly under the shoulders, extend the legs straight (Figure 18.4). Draw the navel inward, protecting the low back, working the core. Keep the elbows tucked against the body. Inhale and lower slowly (Figure 18.5), elbows hugging the sides of the body. Exhale as you lift back up and repeat five times. Note: If you feel any discomfort in the low back, place the knees on the floor. Maintain action in the core; do not let the low back drop down.

Figure 18.4

Figure 18.5

19

ROTATOR CUFFS

General Pose Information: Of the seven muscles that support the shoulder, four are called the rotator cuff. These muscles also support movement of the traps, rhomboids, and pectoralis or chest muscles. In golf, these muscles are responsible for shoulder turn and all shoulder function.

Benefits

- Prevents rotator cuff injuries, one of the most common problems for golfers
- Strengthens the shoulder girdle and also stabilizes the shoulder joint
- Supports greater shoulder turn and club-head speed

Par and Birdie How-To

Par and Birdie #1: Downward-Facing Puppy

Figure 19.1

Begin on all fours, placing hands on the top of the mat. Begin to move buttocks toward the back of the mat (Figure 19.1). Note: Buttocks should not touch the heels, and a 90-degree angle should be maintained at the knee joint.

Figure 19.2

Par and Birdie #2: "Bird Wing" Arms

Elbows are at a 90-degree angle, palms facing up. Elbows must hug the waistline. Inhale and externally rotate arms. Squeeze elbows into the waistline and hold (Figure 19.2). Return to neutral position. Repeat five times.

Eagle How-To

Eagle #1: "Bird Wing" Arms in Warrior B Pose

This pose is an effective way to work the rotator cuff muscles and strengthen the lower body simultaneously. Step the left foot forward; keep the right foot back with the feet a minimum of one leg length apart. The left leg is at a 90-degree angle. The right foot is revolving inward at a 45-degree angle. Draw the navel toward the spine, pressing the left hip forward, stretching the hip flexors and quads (Figure 19.3). Begin five "bird wing" repetitions.

Bogey: The left knee should not extend to more than a 90-degree angle.

Figure 19.3

Eagle #2: Warrior B Pose

Step the left foot forward approximately four feet. Place the right foot at a 45-degree angle. Bend the left knee to a 90-degree angle. Keep the left knee in alignment with the left foot, not collapsing inward. Draw the navel toward the spine, tailbone down, and lift the rib cage. Bring the arms up to roll the shoulders down the back, relaxing the traps (Figure 19.4). Engage the arm and shoulder muscles, creating more strength and support in the shoulders. Hold for five to ten breaths and switch sides.

Figure 19.4

20

CHEST AND THORACIC SPINE

*Few things draw two men together
more surely than a mutual inability to
master golf, coupled with an intense and
ever-increasing love for the game.*
—P. G. WODEHOUSE

General Pose Information: The pectoralis major, or chest, muscles are often in a constantly contracted state due to a sedentary lifestyle and poor posture. We often refer to this condition as "rounded shoulders." Working the thoracic spine supports better posture by addressing the rhomboid and lower trapezius muscles. These muscles also help you to achieve deep thoracic breathing by allowing greater expansion of the diaphragm.

Benefits

- Increases club control
- Supports better posture at address
- Reduces risk of injury
- Increases endurance
- Improves distance off the tee
- Enhances consistency by maintaining a consistent spine angle throughout the swing

Par How-To

Par #1: Standing Chest Opener

Stand with feet hip-width apart. Slightly bend the knees and draw the navel toward the spine, supporting the low back. Clasp the hands behind the back, bringing the fleshy parts of the palms together (Figure 20.1). Roll the shoulders open and hold for five breaths. Fold forward, allowing the hands to come over the head (Figure 20.2). Hold for five breaths.

Figure 20.1

Figure 20.2

Modification: Use a strap, towel, or golf club to bring the hands together behind the back.

Bogey: Continue to draw the navel in toward the spine, but do not arch the low back.

This pose provides an effective, passive stretch for the chest and should be used as an opportunity to work on relaxation and visualization techniques. Use four towels rolled up to accommodate the length of the spine, including the head. Place two towels on the mat at the base of the spine (at the tailbone) and under the head. Place two rolled-up towels under the knees to support the low back. Lie back on the towels, allowing the arms to rest perpendicular to the body, palms facing up (Figure 20.3). You will feel a stretch in the chest muscles. Lie on your back for five minutes, according to your comfort level. Note: Practice this pose in a quiet environment, free from activity, TVs, computers, and ringing phones!

Figure 20.3

Bogey: The buttocks should rest on the mat and the head must be supported by the towels. The neck should not be hyperextended. If you feel discomfort in the low back, reduce the number of towels under your spine.

Birdie How-To

Birdie #1: Chest Opener with Forward Fold

Practice the same chest opener as above with the legs spread wide and feet turned inward. Fold forward over the legs with the knees bent. As you fold forward, bring the arms over the head (Figure 20.4). For additional intensity, begin to straighten the legs. Hold for five to ten breaths.

Bogey: If straightening the legs, do not hyperextend the knees. The body weight should be directly over the middle of the feet, and not too far back. Come out of the pose slowly to avoid light-headedness.

Figure 20.4

Figure 20.5

Birdie #2: Staff Pose

Sit straight or with the back against a wall and the legs out straight. Place the hands by the hips, rolling the shoulders back or pressing the elbows against the wall (Figure 20.5). Use the core as you inhale, draw your navel inward, exhale lifting the rib cage upward, away from the waist. The chest or sternum will begin to move forward.

Bogey: Flex the quadriceps; flex the feet toward the body, and spread the toes. Do not hyperextend the knees.

Eagle How-To
Eagle #1: Locust Pose with Hands Clasped

Lying on your belly with legs together, hands clasped behind the back, engage the buttocks. Bring the legs together as tightly as possible. Draw the navel inward; press the tailbone downward. Roll the shoulders back, chest forward, as the eyes gaze downward. Lift the arms and chest off the floor (Figure 20.6). Hold for five breaths, rest, and repeat three times.

Bogey: Do not hyperextend the neck.

Figure 20.6

21

CORE STRENGTHENING FOR ABDOMINALS

You should want *to hit the ball as far as you can;
don't be ashamed of that.*
—DAVIS LOVE, JR.

General Pose Information: The strength of the abdominals is critical for many aspects of good health. Abdominal, or core strength, supports a healthy back and good posture. The obliques and transverse abdominals initiate rotation in the golf swing.

Benefits

- Supports a straight spine at address and is the stabilizing factor throughout the golf swing
- Supports healthy lumbar spine
- Facilitates better posture
- Supports internal organs
- Essential for trunk rotation and power during the forward motion of the golf swing

Bogey: While practicing crunches, the elbows should remain in the peripheral vision. The head and neck should be supported at all times. Keep the lower spine pressed against the floor, engaging the lower abdominals at all times.

Par How-To

Par #1: Supine Core Strengthening

This pose provides a safe, slow, and effective method for working the abdominals. Note: You will begin to feel relief from low-back pain by practicing this pose daily.

Lie on your back with knees bent. Place a towel between the inner thighs. Inhale, squeeze the towel, and exhale, pressing the navel toward the lumbar spine and the lumbar spine toward the floor (Figure 21.1). Hold for five breaths and repeat three times.

Figure 21.1

Par #2: Supine Core Strengthening with Crunches

With the hands laced behind and supporting the neck, inhale, squeezing the towel. Press the low back toward the floor; exhale, lifting the sternum, and face directly toward the ceiling (Figure 21.2).

Bogey: Do not pull on the neck. Allow the head to rest in the supporting clasped hands.

Figure 21.2

Par #3: Supine Core Strengthening with Crossover Crunches

As you exhale, lift the sternum and face toward the ceiling. Exhale, moving the right shoulder toward the left knee and, then switch sides (Figure 21.3).

Bogey: Keep the elbows in the peripheral vision and do not pull on the neck.

Figure 21.3

Par #4: Yogi Bicycles

Bend the knees, keeping the feet flat on the floor. Keep one foot on the floor, hands behind the head supporting the neck. As you exhale, lift the right shoulder to meet the left knee (Figure 21.4). Switch sides, repeating until the abdominals are fatigued.

Figure 21.4

Birdie How-To

Birdie #1: Lower-Abdominal Crunch

With a rolled-up towel between the inner thighs, lie on your back with the hands laced behind the head. Lift the legs off the floor, maintaining a 90-degree angle. Inhale and press the navel toward the spine, keeping the low back pressed firmly into the floor. Exhale, lifting the legs off the floor and maintaining a 90-degree angle at the hips (Figure 21.5).

Figure 21.5

Birdie #2: Yogi Bicycles

Inhale with one foot off the floor, the other leg extended upward, and the hands behind the head supporting the neck. Exhale, lifting the right shoulder to meet the left knee (Figure 21.6). Switch sides, repeating until the abdominals are fatigued.

Figure 21.6

Figure 21.7

Figure 21.8

Figure 21.9

Birdie #3: Boat Pose with Towel, Knees Bent

Bend the knees and place a towel between the thighs. Place the hands under the thighs to support the back. Draw the navel into the spine, lift the chest, and focus the eyes over the knees. Engage the abdominal section, keeping the spine straight (Figure 21.7). Hold for five breaths.

Bogey: Be aware that there should be no tension on the low back.

Eagle How-To

Eagle #1: Lower-Abdominal Crunch with Towel, Legs Straight

Lifting the legs straight up, flexing feet toward you, squeeze a towel between the knees. Place the hands behind the neck, supporting the head and neck. Inhale and squeeze the towel. Exhale, lifting the hips slightly off the floor and add the upper-body abdominal crunch (Figure 21.8). Note: Keep the elbows in your peripheral vision as you lift the sternum upward. Repeat until fatigued. Exhale during exertion.

Eagle #2: Full Boat Pose

Lift the legs off the floor, legs straight, toes spread wide apart. Engage the quadriceps and draw the navel toward the spine. Arms should be lifted to shoulder height and chest lifted as the abdominals engage. Eyes should focus toward the toes (Figure 21.9). Hold for five to ten breaths. Note: To increase the intensity, place a towel or block between the inner thighs and squeeze the legs together in the pose.

22

CORE STRENGTHENING FOR THE BACK

*Everyone who knows me knows I love music.
I used my music to help me maintain
my swing's rhythm. For me, waltz time or ¾ time
was perfect for the correct golf swing tempo.*
—SAM SNEAD

General Pose Information: The following poses address all areas of the back, from the lumbar spine to the upper trapezius areas. You will not only stretch but also strengthen the back. These poses are suggested as a daily core warm-up sequence. Note: These poses are "mini–back bends" and should be done with special attention to form.

Benefits

- Stretches and strengthens the back muscles; bringing greater elasticity to the spine
- Supports greater rotation
- Supports endurance for a long round of golf
- Provides increased speed and power in the golf swing
- Reduces risk of injury

- Supports effective turn
- Aids digestion and gastric troubles
- Promotes a healthy nervous system

Bogey: Before you begin the back exercises, draw the navel toward the spine and engage the buttocks. This will support the low back, allowing you to move deeper, or increase the intensity in the pose.

Par How-To

Par #1: Cat/Cow Pose (before and after sequence)

Begin on all fours, with hands placed directly under the shoulders. Spread the fingers as wide as possible. As you inhale, draw the navel toward the spine, pressing the spine toward the ceiling as you engage the buttocks. Tuck the chin into the chest, stretching the upper back (Figure 22.1). Exhale, dropping the spine toward the floor, paying attention to pressing the thoracic spine toward the floor, shoulders rolling back (Figure 22.2).

Bogey: Be sure to not hyperextend the neck. Practice this pose ten times, paying attention to coordinating the breath and the movement.

Figure 22.1

Figure 22.2

Par #2: Table Pose with One Leg Extended

Kneeling on all fours, draw the navel toward the spine. Engage the buttocks, pressing the right leg straight back. Flex the foot, keeping toes and hips pointing toward the ground (Figure 22.3). Feel the back and leg muscles working. Hold for five breaths and switch sides.

Par #3: Downward-Facing Puppy (before and after sequence)

This pose can be done in dynamic and static methods. To warm up the low back and shoulders, do the pose dynamically for ten repetitions. Beginning on all fours, inhale while drawing the navel toward the spine, curl the back, and begin to move the buttocks toward the heels (Figure 22.4). As you exhale, bring the body back to the neutral starting position. For more intensity, move into plank position with the upper back slightly arched and shoulders rolling back.

Figure 22.3

For a static posture, begin on all fours and press the buttocks toward the heels. Move the hands toward the top of the mat, spreading the fingers wide, with the shoulders moving away from the ears.

Bogey: You should not feel any discomfort in the knees. If you do, place a blanket between the heels and the buttocks to raise up the buttocks and create more distance at the knee joint. You should also not experience pain in the shoulders.

Figure 22.4

Par #4: Modified Cobra

Lying on the belly, place the hands just below the chest, fingers pointing forward. Be sure the elbows are directly next to the body (like a cricket's hind legs). Inner ankles should be touching with the legs pressed together (Figure 22.5). Inhale, engage the buttocks, press the tailbone down, and begin to telescope the rib cage forward. Keeping the legs on the floor, exhale, slightly lifting the chest off the floor. Hold for five breaths.

Figure 22.5

Bogey: You will feel the back muscles working, but you should not feel pain in the low back.

Birdie How-To

Birdie #1: Extended Table Pose

Figure 22.6

Begin on all fours and draw the navel toward the spine, providing additional support for the back. Inhale and begin by lifting the right leg up, hip pointing toward the floor. Exhale and slowly lift the left arm, extending through the hand (Figure 22.6). Hold for five breaths, lifting the leg and arm as high as possible, then switch sides.

Bogey: Do not arch the back.

Birdie #2: Cobra with Towel

Lie on your belly with a folded towel or block between the upper thighs. Place the hands just below the chest, fingers pointing forward. Be sure the elbows are directly next to the body (like a cricket's hind legs). The inner thighs should grip the prop, automatically engaging the glutes. Press the tailbone down as the rib cage telescopes forward away from the hips. Keeping the legs on the floor, slightly lift the chest off the floor (Figure 22.7). Hold for five breaths.

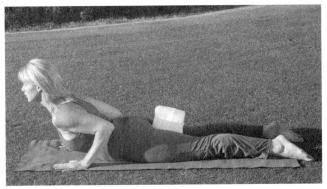

Figure 22.7

Birdie #3: Locust Pose (one hand, one leg up)

Lying on your belly, inhale, draw the navel toward the spine, engage the buttocks, and press the tailbone down. Exhale, lifting the right leg and left arm (Figure 22.8). Hold for five breaths and switch sides.

Figure 22.8

Eagle How-To
Eagle #1: Cobra Push-Ups

Practice the cobra pose with a towel between the thighs, bringing the forearms under the shoulders. Lying on your belly, with the fingers spread wide, exhale and gently lift the chest off the floor. Press the thoracic spine forward, rolling the shoulders back (Figure 22.9). Come back to the starting position. Repeat this "push-up" movement three to five times.

Figure 22.9

Eagle #2: Upward-Facing Dog

Lying on your belly, bring the hands under the shoulders. Draw the navel inward and engage the buttocks and quads. Lift the body up, rolling the shoulders back and chest forward. The thighs should be off the floor, feet active, and fingers spread wide (Figure 22.10). Hold for five breaths.

Bogey: Avoid sinking into or scrunching the shoulders. Lengthen the back of the neck with the eyes focused a few feet in front of the mat.

Figure 22.10

23

LOW BACK

*Most interference originates in the way
we prepare for a shot. The basic point is:
Don't change your swing, change your mind.
Clear the interference, then trust your own
perfect swing, and it will give you
the most consistent results.*
—Joseph Parent

General Pose Information: The number-one injury area for golfers is the low back. The explosive and repetitive nature of the golf swing causes tremendous stress on the low back. The following poses will stretch and strengthen this area. Working the low back should be part of every yoga sequence.

Benefits

- Increases speed in the golf swing
- Increases power and distance
- Reduces risk of injury
- Increases muscular endurance

Par How-To

Par #1: Forward Fold over Chair

Sit in a chair. Spread the legs and allow the body to fold forward (Figure 23.1). Relax the low back. Hold for five breaths.

Figure 23.1

Par #2: Standing Forward Fold with Elbows Clasped and Knees Bent

Figure 23.2

Stand with the feet hip-width apart. Bend the knees and fold forward, allowing the body to hang like a rag doll (Figure 23.2). Hold for five to ten breaths. Come out of this pose slowly to prevent light-headedness, raising one vertebra at a time.

Par #3: Twisting on Chair

Figure 23.3

Sit on the edge of a chair. Inhale, draw the navel inward, and exhale, twisting to one side (Figure 23.3). Hold for five breaths and switch sides.

Par #4: Twisting with Leg on Chair

Stand facing a chair. Bring the left leg up, inhale and draw the navel inward, then exhale, twisting toward the left leg (Figure 23.4). Hold for five breaths and switch sides.

Figure 23.4

Par #5: Supported Eagle Twist with Towel

Lie on your back, arms perpendicular to the body, heels at the buttocks. Cross the right leg over the left and allow the legs to fall to the left. Keep the right shoulder on the floor. To support the back, place a towel under the knees if they do not come to the floor (Figure 23.5). Hold for ten breaths and switch sides.

Figure 23.5

Par #6: Knees into Chest

Lie on your back. Bring one knee into the chest and hold for five breaths (Figure 23.6). Switch sides and then bring both knees onto the chest for five more breaths (Figure 23.7). Relax the head and neck.

Figure 23.6

Figure 23.7

Birdie How-To

Birdie #1: Standing Forward Fold with Elbows Clasped

Start in a standing position. With the legs straight, fold forward and clasp the hands to the opposite elbows (Figure 23.8). Flex the quads and hold for five to ten breaths.

Bogey: Keep the weight over the middle of the foot and not far back in your stance. Keep the toes relaxed.

Figure 23.8

Birdie #2: Spread-Out Hand-to-Block or Club Twist

Stand with the feet wider than hip-width (at least one leg length apart) and feet turned inward. Inhale. Exhale, hinge at the hips, and bring the right hand to the club or to a block on the floor. Twist from the waist to the left, looking over the left shoulder (Figure 23.9). Hold for five breaths and then switch sides.

Figure 23.9

Birdie #3: Dynamic Flow-Eagle Twist

Lie on your back, knees bent, allowing the legs to fall to the right. Inhale and bring the left hand to meet the right hand, allowing the left shoulder to come off the floor (Figure 23.10). Exhale and bring the left arm back perpendicular to the body (Figure 23.11). Continue for five to seven breaths and switch sides.

Figure 23.10

Figure 23.11

Birdie #4: *Crescent Side Stretch*

Stand with feet hip-width apart. Bring the arms above the head, clasping the hands. Engage the leg muscles and buttocks, telescope the rib cage, and stretch to the right (Figure 23.12). Hold for five breaths and switch sides.

Eagle How-To
Eagle #1: *Spread-Out Hand-to-Floor Twist*

Figure 23.12

Stand with the feet wider than hip-width apart (at least one leg length apart) and feet turned inward. Inhale. Exhale, hinge at the hips, and bring the right hand to the floor or a block. Lift the left arm and twist from the waist to the left, looking over the left shoulder (Figure 23.13). Hold for five breaths and switch sides.

Figure 23.13

Figure 23.14

Eagle #2: Standing Rotation with Club

Place the feet in your golf stance, bend the knees, and hinge at
the hips. Maintain proper posture and spine angle, placing a
club behind the shoulder blades. Inhale, engage the core, and
exhale as you begin driving the left shoulder toward the right,
as if taking a backswing (Figure 23.14). Feel the rotation in the
low back and hold for five to ten breaths. Switch sides. Visualize how this rotation will help your golf swing!

Eagle #3

Practice Eagle Poses from Chapter 22, "Core Strengthening for
the Back."

24

HIPS AND GLUTES

Hips initiate the downswing.
They are the pivotal element in the chain reaction.
Starting them first and moving them correctly—
this one action practically
makes the downswing.
—BEN HOGAN

General Pose Information: Tension in the hip and groin area is often a result of sitting for extended periods of time. This constriction of the hip flexors and psoas muscles causes an internal rotation of the pelvis, pulling on the lumbar spine. In addition, lack of flexibility in the hip flexors impedes the ability of the glutes to engage, inhibiting maximum power in the golf swing.

Benefits

- Increases power and distance
- Supports a solid foundation
- Enhances balance
- Enables greater extension in the finish position of the swing sequence
- Increases blood flow to the abdomen, pelvis, and kidneys
- Supports a healthy back
- Increases endurance

Par How-To

Par #1: Modified Pigeon Pose on Back

Figure 24.1

Lying on your back with the knees bent, place your right foot on the outside of your left knee. Press your right knee away from you, flexing the right foot (Figure 24.1). If necessary, wrap a strap or towel around your left thigh and pull the leg toward you. Switch sides and repeat.

Bogey: Relax the head. If the neck is hyperextended, place a towel under the head for additional support.

Par #2: Supported Bound-Angle Pose with Spine Straight

With the back supported by your partner or against a wall, bring the soles of the feet together, allowing the knees to fall outward (Figure 24.2). Draw the navel toward the spine; the hands should clasp the shins as your roll the shoulders back, chest forward. Press the knees toward the floor. You should not feel excessive strain on the inner thighs or groin area.

Figure 24.2

Par #3: Bound-Angle Pose Folding Forward

As you exhale, begin to fold forward, keeping the back flat for as long as possible. Once you have moved to the edge of the pose, allow the spine to round, relaxing the neck and letting the head hang down, releasing any tension (Figure 24.3).

Figure 24.3

Par #4: Modified Bridge Pose

Lie on your back with the knees bent. Inhale and draw the navel toward the spine. Exhale, engage the buttocks, and slowly lift the hips toward the ceiling (Figure 24.4). Feel the extension in the hips and glutes. Hold for five breaths and release, lowering one vertebra at a time.

Figure 24.4

Birdie How-To

Birdie #1: Pigeon Pose on the Floor

Beginning on all fours, bring the right knee to the right wrist (Figure 24.5). With the assistance of the left hand, bring the right lower portion of the leg up toward the front of the mat. Note: You should not feel any tension in the right knee. If so, come out of the pose, and practice Par #1 pose as a modification. Slide the left leg back, moving it away from the front of the mat. Draw the navel toward the spine, protecting the low back, and telescope the rib cage upward. Come high on the fingertips, keeping the chest forward and shoulders back (Figure 24.6). Hold for ten breaths, then switch sides and repeat.

Figure 24.5

Figure 24.6

Birdie #2: Pigeon Pose Folding Forward

Practice the same pose as previously described and fold forward, coming down to the elbows, relaxing the head and neck.

Birdie #3: Bridge Pose with Block

Lie on your back with a block between the knees. Inhale, press the navel toward the spine, engage the buttocks, and rotate the pelvis under. Exhale, squeeze the block, and lift the buttocks higher off the floor than in the Par series (Figure 24.7). Hold for five breaths.

Figure 24.7

Birdie #4: Modified Camel Pose

Kneel on the mat and place the legs hip-width apart. Place the hands on the top of the buttocks, not the low back. Draw the navel inward, telescope the rib cage, and roll the shoulders back. Lift the chest, keeping the chin down, and gently press the buttocks and thighs forward (Figure 24.8). Hold for five breaths and repeat three times.

Bogey: Do not sink into the low back. Focus on lengthening the spine, specifically the thoracic spine.

Figure 24.8

Eagle How-To

Eagle #1: Pigeon Pose with Twist

In the pigeon pose, lean on the left forearm, which should be placed directly under the left shoulder. Lift out of the left shoulder and twist to the right (Figure 24.9). Bring the right hand to the waist or lift the right arm up (Figure 24.10). Hold for five breaths and switch sides.

Figure 24.9

Figure 24.10

Eagle #2: Bridge Pose Without Block

Lie on your back, press the navel toward the spine, and rotate the pelvis under. Engage the buttocks, lift the hips off the floor, and lace the hands together under the back (Figure 24.11). Roll the shoulders under for maximum chest expansion.

Figure 24.11

Eagle #3: Hand-to-Foot Pose with Hip Opening and Twist

Lie on your back with the right hand on the right foot or using a strap, and extend the left leg straight (Figure 24.12). Engage the left quadriceps, inner thigh pressing down, flexing both feet. Hold for five breaths. Extend the right leg out to the right (Figure 24.13). Using the core abdominal strength, keep the left hip on the ground. Hold for five breaths. Place the strap in the left hand and twist the body to the left. Allow the right hip to come off the ground. The arms should remain outstretched, shoulders down (Figure 24.14). Hold for five breaths and switch sides.

Figure 24.12

Figure 24.13

Figure 24.14

25

BALANCING POSES

It is said the eyes are the mirror to the soul.
They also are the mirror to the mind.
With great athletes, their eyes aren't searchlights.
They aren't even spotlights. They are laser beams.
—Gary Mack,
Mind Gym: An Athlete's Guide to Inner Excellence

General Pose Information: If you have ever experienced falling forward or backward in the golf swing you understand the importance of good balance. With age, balance and proprioception (the ability to sense where the body is in space) become compromised. In addition, practicing balancing poses requires one-pointed concentration. The more you can quiet the mind, move inward, and focus on one single point, the easier it becomes to balance. Similarly, in golf, the greater the ability to focus on one task and quiet the mind, the more tension free the swing becomes.

Benefits

- Develops a sense of feeling grounded in the golf stance; a firm connection to the feet
- Supports a consistent swing path
- Reduces extraneous movement in the golf swing; creates more poise and balance

- Quiets the mind
- Teaches one-pointed focus and concentration

Par How-To

Par #1: Tree Pose

Figure 25.1

Select one point of focus on the floor, approximately two feet in front of the mat. Standing with feet hip-width apart, slightly shift the weight onto the left leg, bringing the right foot up to the left ankle, inner knee, or inner thigh, depending on your ability to balance. Bring the hands to the waist for five breaths, then bring the hands above the head for five breaths (Figure 25.1).

Par #2: Supported Dancer Pose

Figure 25.2

Stand and place the left foot in the left hand. Use a club or a chair for balancing support. Press the left quad and hip forward. Keep the knees in line with each other (Figure 25.2). Hold for five to ten breaths. Press the foot into the hand and fold forward slightly as you create space between the buttocks and heel. Hold for five to ten breaths.

Bogey: Keep the abdominals engaged to protect the low back. Do not overarch the back.

Birdie How-To

Birdie #1: Hip-Opening Balance Pose

Figure 25.3

Stand and place the right foot above the left knee, pressing the right knee toward the floor and opening the hip (Figure 25.3). Bend the left knee, draw the navel toward the spine, hinge at the hips, and lower the buttocks toward the floor. Keep the spine flat, with the shoulders rolling back as the arms come up much like airplane wings (Figure 25.4). Focus the eyes approximately three feet in front of you and on one point on the floor. Hold for ten breaths. Switch sides.

Figure 25.4

Eagle How-To

Eagle #1: Full Half-Moon Pose

Place the right hand approximately one foot in front of the right foot. Shift your weight onto the right foot and place the hand on a block or on the floor directly under the shoulder. Begin to shift the weight onto the right leg, lifting the left leg off the floor. (It is acceptable to lift the left leg only an inch or two off the floor.) Begin to open the hips toward the left, rolling the hips open (Figure 25.5). Continue to focus the eyes toward the floor. Hold for five to ten breaths. Note: This pose can be practiced with your back against a wall for support. When you are comfortable, practice the pose without the wall.

Figure 25.5

Eagle #2: Warrior C

Step the right leg forward, placing the hands on the waist or above the head. Imagine the body is one piece, not separated at the waist. Begin to balance on the right leg, bringing the body and left leg parallel to the floor (Figure 25.6). Imagine the letter T. Hold for five to ten breaths and switch sides.

Figure 25.6

26

LEGS

Confidence is everything in golf. . . .
It's confidence that makes a good player into a
great player and eventually a champion.
—FRED COUPLES

General Pose Information: The leg sequencing provides flexibility as well as strength in the legs. In the golf swing, as much as 75 percent of the body weight is distributed to the right side (for right-handed golfers). Strong legs and hips support the body's ability to properly load and generate power and prevent the body from sliding.

Benefits

- Increases push-off power
- Improves power and distance
- Supports a sense of foundation or grounding
- Keeps the right side of the body from sliding
- Assists with better balance
- Strengthens ankles, quads, glutes
- Tones the abdominals

Figure 26.1

Figure 26.2

Par How-To

Par #1: Crescent Warrior Pose with Lunges

From a standing position, step left foot forward, keeping the right leg straight. Keep the left knee at a 45-degree angle. Draw the navel in toward the spine and telescope the rib cage off the waist. Press the right hip forward, increasing the stretch in the hip (Figure 26.1). Inhale and begin to bend the left knee, moving the knee to a 90-degree angle, and exhale as you straighten the right leg. Keep the hands on the waist, or for more intensity raise the arms. Keep the shoulders down, palms facing each other (Figure 26.2). Continue for five to ten repetitions or until muscle failure. Switch sides and repeat.

Par #2: Warrior A

Step the left foot forward approximately four feet or one leg length. Place the right foot on the floor, angled inward at an angle of 90 to 45 degrees. Note: Imagine a line down the middle of the mat. The right foot is to the right of the midline; the left foot is to the left of the midline. Hips must face the front of the mat, not the side. Raise the arms over the head, slightly forward, palms facing each other (Figure 26.3). Hold for five to ten breaths and switch sides.

Bogey: Keep the outer edge of the back foot planted on the floor. Do not roll onto the inside arch of the foot. Draw the navel inward and telescope the rib cage upward. Breathe deeply.

Figure 26.3

Par #3: Warrior B

Step the left foot forward approximately four feet or one leg length. Place the right foot on the floor, angled inward at an angle of 90 to 45 degrees. Note: Imagine a line down the middle of the mat. The right foot is to the right of the midline; the left foot is to the left of the midline. In Warrior B, the hips face slightly to the right. Raise the arms to shoulder height, rolling the shoulder blades together and down the back. Palms should face down, and eyes should focus over the right hand (Figure 26.4). Hold for five to ten breaths and switch sides.

Bogey: Do not shrug the shoulders. Continue to draw the navel toward the spine, telescoping the rib cage.

Figure 26.4

Birdie How-To

Birdie #1: Warrior B, Extended Side-Angle Pose

This pose effectively targets range of motion and provides a strong foundation, opening in the hips, and increased extension. While maintaining the Warrior B pose, begin to bring the left hand or left elbow (depending on your flexibility) down to the left knee. The right arm stretches straight up and, if possible, over the right ear. Extend the arm as much as you can and revolve the rib cage toward the ceiling (Figure 26.5). Hold for five breaths and switch sides. (Note: When I do this pose, I imagine I want to hit the ball twenty yards further so I stretch with 20 percent more intensity!)

Bogey: You may bring your right arm over your head and keep the elbow on the knee.

Figure 26.5

Birdie #2: Standing Quad Stretch
(dancer pose with strap)

Figure 26.6

Balancing on the right leg, bring a strap or towel around the left foot. The palm should face down, fingers pointing away from the body. Keeping the knees in alignment with each other, draw the navel inward and press the hip toward the front of the mat. Press the foot toward the strap, creating more resistance in the quadriceps (Figure 26.6). Hold for five breaths and switch sides.

Bogey: Keeping the knees in alignment will reduce the risk of pain in the knee joint. If you feel discomfort in the knee, loosen the strap.

Birdie #3: Chair Pose

Figure 26.7

Start in a standing position, then bring the feet and knees together. Inhale and begin to bend the knees, hinging at the hips as if preparing to sit in a chair. Draw the navel in, tuck the tailbone under, and shift your weight toward the heels. Exhale, bringing the hands to the waist or lifting the arms with palms facing each other (Figure 26.7). Hold for five breaths.

Birdie #4: Standing Quad Stretch (dancer pose with club)

Practice the standing quad stretch described above supported by a golf club (Figure 26.8). Hold for five breaths and switch sides.

Figure 26.8

Eagle How-To

Eagle #1: Revolving Side-Angle Pose

From a standing position, step the right foot forward into a crescent-lunge position and place the left knee on the floor. Bring the left elbow to the outside of the right knee. Place the left hand into a fist position with the right palm resting on top. Press the left arm into the right knee, lifting out of the left shoulder (Figure 26.9). Focus on twisting from the core to the shoulders, eyes focused on the floor. For more lower body intensity, curl the left toes under, bringing the left knee off the floor while holding the left leg straight. Hold for five breaths and switch sides.

Figure 26.9

27

HAMSTRINGS

eneral Pose Information: The most common physical complaint among golfers is low-back pain. Obviously the repetitive, explosive nature of the golf swing causes strain on the low back, but there are many physical elements that contribute to lumbar spine problems, including tight hamstrings.

Benefits
- Supports a strong foundation
- Enhances balance in a bad lie
- Reduces incidence of back injury
- Maintains knee flexion at the address position

Par How-To
Par #1: Staff Pose with Strap

Sit up straight (feel free to bring the back against a wall) with a strap around the feet, legs extended out. Inhale and draw the navel toward the spine; exhale, engaging the quadriceps and flexing the feet toward the body (Figure 27.1). Hold for five to ten breaths and repeat three times.

Bogey: Although you will feel the hamstrings working, do not go to the point of pain. Remember to breathe deeply, visualizing the hamstrings releasing.

Figure 27.1

Par #2: Head-to-Knee Pose

Sitting on the mat, bring the sole of the right foot to the inner thigh of the left leg. Square the hips and chest directly over the left leg. Inhale deeply, bringing the arms over the head, and exhale as you fold forward over the left leg (Figure 27.2). Hold for five breaths.

Bogey: Remember that less is more. There is a greater value in moving half the distance in the pose and holding it for a longer duration.

Figure 27.2

Par #3: Lying-Down Hand-to-Foot Pose with Strap

Lie on your back and wrap a strap or towel around the lifted right foot. Keep the left leg bent and draw the navel toward the spine. Maintain a completely straight right leg, engaging the right quadriceps, flexing the foot toward you, and pressing the heel away from you (Figure 27.3). Hold for five breaths and switch sides.

Figure 27.3

Par #4: Modified Crescent-Lunge Pose

From a standing position, step the right foot forward, positioning the knee at a 90-degree angle. Allow the left knee to come to the ground, leaning into the left hip. Inhale, drawing the navel toward the spine and telescoping the rib cage upward, with the shoulders rolled back and chest forward (Figure 27.4). Exhale, moving to the edge of the pose, feeling the stretch in the hip flexors and quads but not in the low back. Hold for five breaths and switch sides.

Figure 27.4

Birdie How-To

Birdie #1: Staff Pose Folding Forward

Figure 27.5

Practice the staff pose described above without the strap and fold forward as much as possible in the pose (Figure 27.5). Relax the head and neck.

Bogey: Place the hands on the outsides of the legs or the feet. Do not scrunch the shoulders by reaching too intensely for the feet.

Birdie #2: Lying-Down Hand-to-Foot Pose with Strap and with the Leg Extended

Figure 27.6

Lie on your back and wrap a strap or towel around the lifted right foot. Extend the left leg toward the floor. Press the right heel toward the ceiling lifting the leg as high as possible to deepen this pose (described in Par #3). Flex the left quad and foot, paying attention to flexing the adductors, or inner thigh muscles (Figure 27.6). Keep the right leg as close to the floor as necessary to keep it straight. Hold for ten breaths and switch sides.

Birdie #3: Downward-Facing Dog

Figure 27.7

Beginning on all fours with fingers spread wide, walk the hands toward the front of the mat. Slowly lift the hips, shifting the weight into the legs, pressing the spine long, and pushing the mat away from you. Straighten the legs, moving the heels toward the floor (Figure 27.7). Note: If the hamstrings are tight, slightly bend the knees.

Bogie: The heels will eventually move toward the floor, but do not shorten the distance between the hands and feet to get the heels down. Envision a pyramid shape as the optimum position.

Eagle How-To

Eagle #1: Triangle

From a standing position, step out the left foot three to four feet, placing the foot so it is parallel to the edge of the mat. Revolve the right leg inward, with the foot placed at an angle of 90 to 45 degrees. Inhale and begin to draw the navel inward, telescoping the rib cage and lengthening the left side of the body over the left leg. Exhale and place the hand on the left leg, revolving the rib cage toward the ceiling with the right arm stretching upward (Figure 27.8). Eyes should focus up toward the right hand or, if there is tension in the neck, look to the floor. Flex the quads and adductors. Hold for five to ten breaths and switch sides.

Bogey: Keep the toes relaxed but lift in the arches.

Figure 27.8

Eagle #2: Lying-Down Hand-to-Foot Pose with Both Legs Extended

Practice this pose as described in Birdie #2, but with both legs extended fully. Press the right heel toward the ceiling, lifting the leg as high as possible to deepen this pose (described in Par #3). Flex the left quad and foot, paying attention to flexing the adductors, or inner thigh muscles (Figure 27.9). Keep the right leg as close to the floor as necessary to keep it straight. Hold for ten breaths and switch sides.

Figure 27.9

28

POSES FOR BETTER BREATHING

General Pose Information: Deep diaphragmatic and thoracic breathing is affected by the capacity of the rib cage to expand and contract. The lats, pecs, serratus anterior, and intercostal muscles all affect the body's capacity for breathing.

Benefits

- Increases energy
- Calms the mind
- Relieves tension in the body and mind
- Enhances rhythm and tempo in the swing
- Supports endurance

Par How-To

Par #1: Crescent Side Bends

Inhale, lifting the right arm and feeling the stretch from the hip up through the fingertips. Exhale, pressing the left arm down to increase the intensity (Figure 28.1). Hold for five breaths and switch sides.

Figure 28.1

Par #2: Standing Chest Opener

Standing with feet hip-width apart, slightly bend the knees and draw the navel toward the spine, supporting the low back. Clasp the hands behind the back, bringing the fleshy parts of the palms together (see Figures 20.1 and 20.2 on page 92). Roll the shoulders open and hold for five breaths.

Modification: Use a strap, towel, or golf club to bring the hands together behind the back.

Par #3: Alligator Twists

Lying on the back, bring the left foot to the right knee; arms should be perpendicular to the body, palms facing up. Twist the left side of the body, including the hip, over to the right (Figure 28.2). Turn the head to the left to increase the intensity. Hold for ten to fifteen breaths, allowing gravity to deepen the pose. Concentrate on the expansion of the rib cage. Switch sides and repeat.

Figure 28.2

Birdie #1: Bridge Pose Without Block

Lying on your back, inhale, pressing the navel toward the spine and rotate the pelvis under. Engage the buttocks, exhale, lift the hips off the floor, and lace the hands together under the back, arms straight. Roll the shoulders under for maximum chest expansion (Figure 28.3).

Figure 28.3

29

RELAXATION AND VISUALIZATION

*The Zone, a mystical state of consciousness
that seems to be neither physical nor mental—
effortless amid tense exertion—as if playing in
slow motion—perceptually sharp, keenly alert, with
heightened concentration—almost as if being psychic.
Such profound experiences, often commonplace to athletes,
bear comparison to daydreaming, communion
with nature, and spiritual contemplation.*
—GARY GACH,
The Complete Idiot's Guide to Buddhism

Relaxation pose or corpse pose is the most important part of the yoga practice, second only to breathing. This pose is practiced at the end of the yoga sequence and should never be skipped. If you are short on time, it is more beneficial to take the time for the relaxation or corpse pose than it is to do more poses. This is the period when the nervous system incorporates all the work you have just done, allows the body to rest, and offers the mind an opportunity to imprint the mental intentions so important to golf and life.

The concept of "conscious relaxation" is often disputed among yogis. In the corpse pose, although we are completely relaxed, the mind is still "awake." You want to remain "gently conscious," being present in the pose.

Setting Up for Corpse Pose

Option one: Lie on your back and place towels under your knees. Begin by contracting every muscle in the body. Hold for two breaths and relax on the exhalation (Figure 29.1).

Option two: In corpse pose, begin visualizing tension leaving your body. Begin from the toes and move to the crown of the head. Each exhalation relieves tension, sinking you deeper into the ground.

You can let your mind rest, allowing the mind to drift and flow freely, or take this time to practice the visualization techniques so important to golf performance.

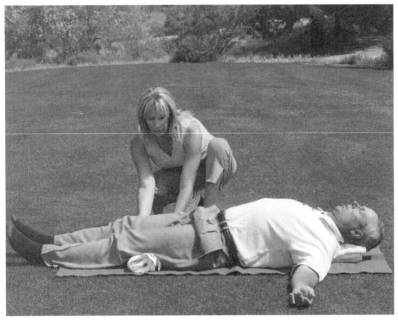

Figure 29.1

30

IN THE
LOCKER ROOM

Without a comprehensive understanding of the science of strength and conditioning, the golfer who attempts conditioning to enhance performance is likely to seek help from a bookstore or a local personal trainer. Having followed the advice from either source, many golfers find an improvement in their ability to walk from hole to hole without getting winded, yet are dismayed when there is no improvement in their golf game. The inevitable downside is the neglect of flexibility and strength conditioning to improve performance.

When golfers train using exercise programs based on bodybuilding principles, sedation of the nervous system's ability to organize and synchronize complex multijoint movements is inevitable. This result is the complete opposite of what a golfer needs to improve function!

Letting Go

Have you ever noticed the tension in the face and body of someone who always needs to be in control? Control and tension are the antithesis of letting go. Nothing restricts a fluid golf swing faster than tension in the mind and body.

Recently I was playing in a golf tournament comprised of golf writers. We had the opportunity to play five beautiful courses in Scottsdale in five days. Between the on-course trials and tribulations and the nineteenth-hole antics, we bonded in a short period of time.

During the third day of play, I found myself on the seventh hole in a deep bunker, and I mean deep! Forget seeing the green, I couldn't even see the flag! As I stood in the bunker, I took out my cell phone (very bad manners, which should not be repeated on any golf course) and called my friend, who had helped design the golf course. I asked his advice for getting out of this dilemma. I begged for help: "How do I get out of this bunker?" I anticipated a comment such as, "Forget the bunker, Katherine, and just give up the game." Fortunately, my friend is known for his quick wit. "Hand wedge, Katherine, just use the hand wedge." His advice went further, with detailed instructions on releasing the sand from my left hand strategically timed at the "impact" of the club on the sand.

After our conversation, I put the cell phone back in the cart and grabbed my sand wedge. Usually this bunker shot has my heart racing and my blood pressure rising at its ridiculous difficulty. As I stepped into the bunker, something in me shifted. I felt completely calm, assured that I had the ability to make this shot. I hit the ball, sending it soaring out of the bunker with authority and grace and landing four feet from the hole.

When I let go of the fear, I moved into a place of confidence, a sense of knowing. I said to myself, "Let's have some fun here. This shot does not define me as a person." And I began to let go of the outcome.

Letting go does not equal apathy, indifference, or brashness. Letting go means you make a conscious choice to do your best, step up to the ball, breathe, and let go of what you can no longer control.

Between changing into your golf shoes and hitting the range, practicing the following six yoga poses with the assistance of a chair will help prepare you for the round. Before you begin stretching, do some deep breathing while standing with the feet hip-width apart. Breathing will increase blood flow to the muscles, preparing the body for the yoga poses. Start by inhaling, bringing the arms over the head. Feel the rib cage expanding as you lengthen in the waist. Exhale, lowering the arms down. Repeat five to ten times.

Figure 30.1

Seated Forward Fold

Sitting on the edge of the chair, legs apart, allow the body to fold forward, releasing any tension in the low back. Let the head hang down, releasing tension in the neck (Figure 30.1). Hold for five to ten breaths. Come out of the pose slowly so you do not feel light-headed.

Standing Rhomboid Stretch

Standing, place feet slightly wider than hip-width apart. Bend the knees and draw the navel toward the spine, supporting the back. Lace the hands together in front of the body and drop the arms slightly lower than shoulder height. Press the hands and arms away from the upper body. Feel the stretch in the upper back. Increase the intensity by tucking the chin toward the chest (Figure 30.2). Hold for ten breaths.

Figure 30.2

Figure 30.3

Standing Twist with Foot on Chair, Transitioning into Forward Fold

Face the chair and place your left foot on the chair; the right leg is straight, with the heel lifted or flat on the floor. Be sure the left knee is not at more than a 90-degree angle (Figure 30.3). Draw the navel toward the spine, telescoping the rib cage upward. Engage the buttocks on the right side, pressing the right hip toward the chair. Begin to twist toward the left. Now straighten the left leg and fold forward (Figure 30.4). Feel the stretch in the left hip and hold for five to ten breaths. Switch sides and repeat.

Figure 30.4

Standing Chest Opener

Stand with feet hip-width apart. Slightly bend the knees and draw the navel toward the spine, supporting the low back. Clasp the hands behind the back, bringing the fleshy parts of the palms together (Figure 30.5). Roll the shoulders open and hold for five breaths. Fold forward, allowing the hands to come over the head. Hold for five breaths.

Figure 30.5

Standing Quad Stretch

Balancing on the right leg, place the left foot in the left hand. Keeping the knees in alignment with each other, draw the navel inward and press forward. Press the foot toward the hand, creating more resistance in the quadriceps and hip flexors (Figure 30.6). Hold for five breaths and switch sides.

Figure 30.6

Standing Twist with Club Behind Shoulders

Standing with feet wider than hip-width apart (simulating the golf stance), tilt at the hips, placing a golf club directly behind the shoulder blades. Draw the navel in, telescope the rib cage up, and inhale deeply. Exhale, twisting the left shoulder toward the right side and look downward (Figure 30.7). Hold on the right side for five to ten breaths. Visualize the desired rotation in your backswing. Slowly release out of the pose, move to the other side, and hold for five to ten breaths (Figure 30.8). Visualize the perfect finish position.

Figure 30.7

Figure 30.8

31

ON THE GOLF COURSE

The "first-tee" stretch sequence uses the golf cart and golf clubs. This sequence should be done before, during, and after the round. Keep the muscles loose by stretching continuously throughout the round. You will be more consistent, experience more speed and power in your swing, and maintain the necessary endurance.

Standing Cat/Cow Pose

Warming up the low back reduces the risk of injury and supports a consistent, powerful swing plane. Placing the hands on the cart about shoulder height, begin to walk the legs back. Inhale and draw the navel inward, curling the back just as in the cat/cow pose (Figure 31.1). Begin to exhale, allowing the body to hang against the weight of the golf cart (Figure 31.2). Inhale and come back to the original position. Repeat five times and then hold the pose in the fully extended position for five breaths. Use the force of gravity to deepen the pose.

Figure 31.1

Figure 31.2

Figure 31.3

Downward-Facing Dog with Golf Cart

This pose warms up the shoulders, low back, hamstrings, and Achilles tendons. It also supports push-off power and a solid foundation. Facing the front of the cart, place the hands wider than shoulder-width apart. Step the feet back, creating a 90-degree angle in the hips. Roll the shoulders back away from the ears and flex the quads (Figure 31.3). Hold for five breaths.

Figure 31.4

Shoulder-Rotation Twist Pose

This pose increases shoulder turn and reduces the risk of shoulder injury. Standing perpendicular to the cart, place the arms on the vertical support of the cart. Separate the hands to increase the stretch in the shoulders (Figure 31.4). Use the abdominals by drawing the navel inward for more intensity and core conditioning. Hold for five breaths. Switch sides and repeat.

Warrior Crescent Lunge

This pose works the hip flexors, psoas, quads, and glutes, giving more extension and power by supporting full hip extension. Bringing the left leg onto the back of the cart, come up onto the right toes (Figure 31.5). Engage the right buttocks and press the right hip toward the cart.

Figure 31.5

Head-to-Knee Pose

Hamstring flexibility has a direct correlation to keeping the low back healthy. Begin by stepping the left foot on the cart. Straighten the left leg and flex the left foot and quad. Keep the hips and chest squared off, facing the left knee. Hinge at the hips, folding forward (Figure 31.6). Hold for five breaths and repeat, beginning with the crescent pose on the right side.

Figure 31.6

Eagle Arms with Club

Bring the right arm up, palm facing you. Let the right forearm fall behind the back, grabbing the golf club. Bring the left arm behind you, grabbing onto the same club (Figure 31.7). Feel the stretch in the shoulders. Hold for five breaths and switch sides.

Figure 31.7

Figure 31.8

Figure 31.9

Standing Rotational Twist

This pose increases the range of motion in the swing. Step the left foot forward, hips squared to the feet. Draw the navel inward and telescope the rib cage, placing the right hand on the golf cart. Use the strength of the legs to create a solid foundation and twist from the waist (Figure 31.8). Birdie: Keep the left hand on the waist. Eagle: Bring the left arm up and focus over the left hand (Figure 31.9). Hold for five breaths and switch sides.

Figure 31.10

Seated Twist

This is a great pose to keep the core and shoulders loose—a great one to do at every hole! Sitting up as straight as possible, bring the body to the edge of the seat. Draw the navel toward the spine and begin to twist from the hips, not just the shoulder. Bring the left hand to the right knee and the right hand behind you to increase the intensity. Twist deeper with each exhalation (Figure 31.10). Hold for five breaths and switch sides.

Acceptance

Ruth was playing team matches at her country club one day when she experienced a very humbling moment. "The elevated first tee was twenty-five steep steps straight up. My opponent was an elderly lady (fifty-five years old—I was thirty-five), and I thought I had the match in the bag as I watched her struggle to make it up the steps.

"As the country club member my opponent had the 'honors' to hit first. She took her driver out and hit the ball 150 yards, landing it in the middle of the fairway. Knowing that my drives average 200 yards I was feeling very confident. I was younger and stronger, and I rarely hit the ball out of the fairway. I had the match! I was happy when my teammate and I made eye contact across the fairway—I let her know the match was mine, no worries.

"I took the driver out of my bag and made several practice swings (incidentally, my opponent took no practice swings), and I proceeded to hit the ball very high. I sliced to the right and the ball landed amidst the trees between two very deep roots.

"My caddie, who taught me the value of using a three wood on the green, had already gained my respect (one cannot underestimate the value of the bump and run shot). He suggested I take my four iron and hit the ball backward, hoping to get it out into the fairway. He graciously 'suggested' that as soon as I hit the ball, I should duck to avoid getting hit in the face. Like a new recruit, I followed his instructions to a tee. I 'smacked' the ball and it landed fifty yards behind my opponent's first shot. So there I was, lying in three. I was glad my teammates were not close by—I would have to have shown the thumbs down.

"Being a consummate competitor, I congratulated my opponent after the round and directed her to the nineteenth hole where I usually ordered a Virgin Mary or a diet Coke. Today, I ordered a double gin and tonic—light on the tonic.

"On the way home I tried to evaluate my grip, my right elbow (which seemed to have a mind of its own), my takeaway, and my follow-through, but something more meaningful happened. I realized that I truly respected this 'elderly' lady (I am seventy-five years old now) and decided to work on my game with a shift in my focus. I do not think about my game in the same way I used to think about it, as a mechanical process. Now I view my game with more spirit and acceptance. I want more enjoyment, plain and simple. I made a conscious decision to see the beauty of the course, feel the ground beneath me, and appreciate the beauty. Now I hear the birds, smell the freshly cut grass, and love and live in the moment. Oddly enough, my game got better and forty years later I still enjoy the game.

"Although I remained a high-handicap golfer, I am a much happier golfer."

32

YOUR SEQUENCES: FIFTEEN, THIRTY, AND FORTY-FIVE MINUTES

People often ask me,
"Why can't I play golf the same every day?"
Well, what can you do the same every day?
I don't even get out of bed the same way.
—JACKIE BURKE, JR.

Before beginning any longer sequencing, always begin with your warm-up sequence, which takes approximately fifteen minutes. If time allows, provide at least five to ten minutes for the relaxation pose. After you become familiar with your practice, it is acceptable to add a few poses specific to your needs. Feel free to vary the sequences. For example, I suggest you practice with one sequence on Monday, Wednesday, and Friday and use a second or varied sequence for Tuesdays and Thursdays.

Fifteen-Minute Yoga Practice
Par Sequence

Figure 32.1
Chest-opener pose

Figure 32.2
Crescent
side-stretch pose

Figure 32.3
Spread-out hand-to-foot
pose with block

Figure 32.4
Supported dancer pose

Figure 32.5
Core-strengthening
abdominals pose
with crunches

Figure 32.6
Bound-angle pose folding forward

Figure 32.7
Alligator twist

Figure 32.8
Relaxation

Birdie Sequence

Figure 32.9 a–b Chest opener with forward fold

Figure 32.10
Eagle arms in Warrior B pose

Figure 32.11
Triangle pose

Figure 32.12
Bound-angle pose
folding forward

Figure 32.13
Pigeon pose

Figure 32.14
Alligator twist

Figure 32.15
Relaxation

Eagle Sequence

Figure 32.16 a–b Chest opener with a
forward fold

Figure 32.17
Triangle pose

Figure 32.18
Warrior B with extended
side-angle pose

Figure 32.19
Core strengthener—
modified boat pose
with towel

Figure 32.20
Lying down hand-to-foot
pose with twist

Figure 32.21
Relaxation

Thirty-Minute Yoga Practice
Par Sequence

Figure 32.22 a–b
Crescent warrior pose with lunges

Figure 32.23
Triangle pose

Figure 32.24
Tree pose

Figure 32.25
Modified pigeon pose

Figure 32.26
Bound-angle pose

Figure 32.27
Supine core-strengthening
with crunches

Figure 32.28
Extended table pose

Figure 32.29
Bridge pose with block

Figure 32.30
Relaxation

Birdie Sequence

Figure 32.31
Warrior A pose

Figure 32.32
Triangle pose

Figure 32.33
Warrior B pose

Figure 32.34
Extended side-angle pose

Figure 32.35 a–b
Hip-opening balance pose

Figure 32.36
Supine core-strengthening
with crunches

Figure 32.37
Extended table pose

Figure 32.38
Pigeon pose on the floor

Figure 32.39
Alligator twist

Figure 32.40
Relaxation

Eagle Sequence

Figure 32.41 a–b Warrior poses

Figure 32.42 a–b
Hip-opening balance pose

Figure 32.43
Spread-out hand-to-floor-with-twist pose

Figure 32.44 a–b Half-moon pose

Figure 32.45
Revolving side-angle pose

Figure 32.46
Yogi bicycles

Figure 32.47
Boat pose

Figure 32.48
Head-to-knee pose

Figure 32.49 a–b Pigeon pose with twist

Figure 32.50
Bridge pose without block

Figure 32.51
Lying-down extended
hand-to-foot twist

Figure 32.52
Relaxation

Forty-Five-Minute Sequence

Add three to five Sun Salutations to the beginning of each of the thirty-minute sequences as shown in Chapter 13. Allow ten minutes for the relaxation pose.

33

POSTROUND RESTORATIVE SEQUENCE

Postround stretching helps the musculosckeletal system recover from the taxing physical effects of golf, reduces the onset of soreness, and lowers the risk of injury. The term *restorative* refers to the body's ability to restore itself to its original, healthy condition.

All restorative or postround poses should be practiced at a moderate level of intensity. Close the eyes, play soft, soothing music if possible, and relax. When the mind and body are relaxed, one is open to conscious as well as subliminal or unconscious thoughts. As we discussed in the chapter on meditation, visualization plays a key role in predicting the desired outcome. Take this time to practice visualizing your body flexible and strong, with your mind "in the zone" with your optimum golf-swing pattern.

Twist Supported by Blankets Under the Knees

Lie on your back with the arms perpendicular to the body. Bend the knees and bring the heels close to the buttocks. Allow the

Figure 33.1

knees to fall to the left, resting the knees on two to three rolled-up towels. Keep the right shoulder on the ground (Figure 33.1). Adjust the height of the towels for the desired twist; for less intensity, raise the number of towels under your knees. You should feel a gentle stretch in the low back, rib cage, and chest area. This pose supports the range of motion in the low back and passively stretches the intercostals.

Supported Bridge Pose with Block

Figure 33.2

Lie on your back, knees bent, with the heels close to the buttocks. Draw the navel toward the spine and lift the hips up. Place a block or two to three towels under the tailbone. Be sure the block is placed low toward the sacrum and *not* under the middle back (Figure 33.2). You should not feel any discomfort in the low back. Place the arms by your sides, palms facing up. Allow the body to rest on the towels. This pose works the hip flexors and facilitates blood flow from the heart to the brain.

Legs up the Wall or Resting on a Chair

Lying on your back, bring the buttocks as close to a wall as possible or to the legs of a chair. Bring the body around so the legs rest on the seat of the chair (Figure 33.3) or against the wall or

Figure 33.3

Figure 33.4

chair (Figure 33.4). If the legs are on the wall, the hips should be on the floor and not elevated. If necessary, place a small towel under the head so the neck is not hyperextended. Place the arms next to the body, palms facing up. This pose offsets the effects of the round in the lower extremities. You will feel relief in the knees and feet, reducing swelling and joint pain.

Chest Opener with Bolster or Towels Under the Spine

Using four towels, take two and roll them up like a jelly roll cake to accommodate the entire length of your spine, sacrum to the head. Note: Be sure the head is supported when you lie back.

Take the remaining towels, rolling them up to be placed under your knees. Sitting on the mat, place the "jelly roll" at the base of the spine. Place the other towels under the knees. Roll back onto the towels feeling the opening in the chest, palms face up (Figure 33.5). Be sure the head is supported and there is no discomfort in the lumbar spine. Relax for three to five minutes. To come out of the pose, roll over to the right side for thirty seconds before standing up. Note: Let gravity do the work in these poses. Breathe deeply and rest. Try to hold each pose approximately three to five minutes.

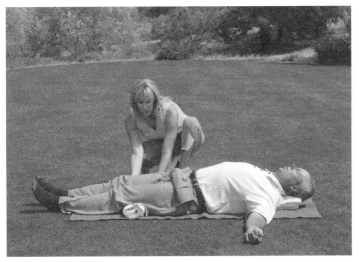

Figure 33.5

A CLOSING
MEDITATION

Close your eyes and you will see clearly.
Cease to listen and you will hear truth.
Be silent and your heart will sing.
Seek no contacts and you will find union.
Be still and you will move forward on the tide of the spirit.
Be gentle and you will need no strength.
Be patient and you will achieve all things.
Be humble and you will remain entire.
　　　　　—Taoist meditation

GLOSSARY OF YOGA TERMS

Asana Exercise posture.

Ashram Typically secluded community where yoga is practiced.

Ashtanga A hatha yoga practice that emphasizes strength and intense stretching; an athletic style sometimes referred to as power yoga.

Ayurveda Ancient holistic Indian medical system of health and well-being with an emphasis on the individual's involvement.

Guru Yoga master or teacher.

Hatha Yogic system of balancing the body's energies; includes asanas.

Iyengar Hatha yoga practice with emphasis on alignment and structure.

Kundalini The body's energy that is found coiled at the base of the spine. Kundalini yoga uses breathing, sound, and meditation as its major resources.

Namaste Sanskrit word meaning "I salute the spirit in you." Traditional Indian and Nepalese greeting.

Niyama Yogic text on how to treat yourself.

Om Origin of all sound, a sacred symbol. Vibration of the *om* sound centers the body and aligns energy.

Patanjali Author of the *Yoga Sutras*, the comprehensive text on the yoga system.

Pranayama Rhythmic control of breathing used to increase prana or energy and reduce obstructions in the body and mind.

Sanskrit The ancient language of Hinduism and the classical literary language of India.

Ujjayi breathing Deep and audible breathing exercise; utilizes diaphragmatic breathing, which enhances athletic performance.

Vinyasa The flowing style of yoga; an asana that links poses together.

Yama Ethical disciplines for how to treat others.

Yoga Literally means "to yoke"—to bring together, or union. A system of healing and self-transformation based in wholeness and unity.

Yoga Sutras A compilation of writings by Patanjali that is considered the most comprehensive and fundamental text on the system of yoga.

Yogi Practitioner of yoga.

Yogin Male yogi.

Yogini Female yogi.

RESOURCES

Yoga Links

    www.yogadirectory.org
    www.yogajournal.com
    www.yoganet.org
    www.yogasite.org

Golf Links

    www.TheGolfChannel.com
    www.golfonline.com
    www.golfinstruction.com
    www.PGA.com

Golf Biomechanical Information

    Paul Chek, M.S.S., H.H.P., N.M.T.
    The C.H.E.K. Institute
    609 South Vulcan, Suite 101
    Encinitas, CA 92024
    www.chekinstitute.com

    Jeff Banaszak, P.T., C.S.C.S.
    Back 9 Fitness
    P.O. Box 20336
    Bradenton, FL 34204-0336
    (941) 756-9211
    (877) 469-9865 (toll free)
    Fax: (941) 756-9212
    www.back9fitness.com

Women's Golf Apparel
Nike Golf
www.nikegolf.com

Kitten with Her Sticks
Teresa Gutierrez
www.kittenwithhersticks.com

BIBLIOGRAPHY

Andrisani, John. *The Tiger Woods Way: Secrets of Tiger Woods' Power-Swing Technique*. New York: Crown Publishers, 1997.

Chek, Paul. *The Golf Biomechanic's Manual*. Vista, CA: C.H.E.K. Institute, 1999, 2001.

Coulter, H. David. *Anatomy of Hatha Yoga, A Manual for Students, Teachers and Practicioners*. Honesdale, PA: Body and Breath, Inc., 2002.

Feurerstein, Georg, Ph.D. and Larry Payne, Ph.D. *Yoga for Dummies*. New York: John Wiley & Sons, IDG Books, 1999.

Gach, Gary. *The Complete Idiot's Guide to Buddhism*. Indianapolis, IN: Alpha Books, Pearson Education, Inc., 2002.

Iyengar, B.K.S. *Yoga—The Path to Holistic Health*. London: Dorling Kindersley, 2001.

Mack, Gary. *Mind Gym: An Athlete's Guide to Inner Excellence*. New York: McGraw-Hill, 2001.

Parent, Joseph. *Zen Golf*. New York: Doubleday, 2002.

Price, Nick. *The Swing: Mastering the Principles of the Game*. New York: Random House, 1997.

Sieg, Kay W. and Sandra P. Adams. *Illustrated Essentials of Musculoskeletal Anatomy*, Third Edition. Gainesville, FL: Mega Books, 1996.

Voorhees, Randy. *As Hogan Said . . . The 389 Best Things Ever Said about How to Play Golf*. New York: Mountain Lion, Inc., Simon and Schuster, 2000.

INDEX